DIVING
MICRONESIA

DIVING
MICRONESIA
By Eric Hanauer

AQUA QUEST PUBLICATIONS, INC. ■ NEW YORK

PUBLISHER'S NOTE

The Aqua Quest *Diving* series offers extensive information on dive sites as well as topside activities.

At the time of publication, the information contained in this book was determined to be as accurate and up-to-date as possible. The reader should bear in mind, however, that dive site terrain and landmarks change due to weather or construction. In addition, new dive shops, restaurants, hotels and stores can open and existing ones close. Telephone numbers are subject to change as are government regulations.

The publisher welcomes the reader's comments and assistance to help ensure the accuracy of future editions of this book.

Good diving and enjoy your stay!

Library of Congress Cataloging-in-Publication Data

Hanauer, Eric
    Diving Micronesia / by Eric Hanauer.
        p. cm.
    Includes index.
    ISBN 1-881652-19-X : $18.95 (alk. paper)
    1. Scuba diving—Micronesia—Guidebooks. 2.
    Micronesia—Guidebooks. I. Title. II. Series
GV838.673.M625 H25 2000
919.6504—dc21
                            00-058269

Cover: Fabios Amaral's light illuminates the 16-inch guns beneath the upside-down bow of the Japanese battleship *Nagato* at 165 feet (50 m) at Bikini Atoll.

Title page: Gray reef sharks cruise at Shark Reef, Bikini Atoll.

Printed in Hong Kong
10 9 8 7 6 5 4 3 2 1

Design by Richard Liu.

ACKNOWLEDGEMENTS

Any outsider coming into an area to write a guidebook is greatly dependent on the help of local residents. The warmth of Micronesia was amply demonstrated by people from all walks of life who helped bring this project to fruition. To all of them, and to anyone I may have inadvertently forgotten, my sincere thanks:

Marshall Islands: Fabio Amaral, Jack Niedenthal, Peter Gigante, Collette Reimers, Ramsey Reimers, Ronnie Reimers, Layne Ballard, Steve Gavegan, Matt Holly, Carl Douglas, Lennie Blix, Leigh Tobin; Kosrae: Doug and Sally Beitz, Geoff Raaschou, Madison Nena, Goro Sekiguchi, Max Mongeya, Marcellus Elly, Grant Ismael, Roger Emerson, Mike Collins, Katrina Adams, Donald Jonah; Pohnpei: Yukio and Ritsuko Suzuki, Emensio Eperiam, Patti Arthur, Dr. Steve Auerbach; Guam: Cathy Gogue, Jim Nelson, Pete Peterson, Tim Rock, Mary Radcliffe-Gicca, John Morvant, Valerie Paul, Jim Brandt, Leto Bautista; Saipan: Ben Concepcion, Ed and Jeannie Comfort, James Matsumoto, Tom Goresch, Rick Northen; Rota: Mark and Lynne Michael, Joel Naguit, Jon Pearlman, Doug Skilang; Yap: Bill and Patricia Acker, Leo Ragman, Jesse Faimaw, Dave Vecella; Palau: Francis Toribiong, David Feinberg, Lee Bachelor, Cary Dale, Sam Scott; Truk: Kimiuo and Gradvin Aisek, Clay Wiseman, Rainer Kinney, Clark Graham, Estos, Chenni, Charlie Arneson; USA: Mia Tegner, Ken Loyst, Tony Bliss, Layne Ballard, Christie Radican, Rick Thom, Claude Smith.

DEDICATION
To the memory of Mia Tegner—
marine biologist, environmentalist, diver, adventurer
My wife, lover, companion, best friend

CONTENTS

FOREWORD

This book is the first comprehensive diver's guide to all the islands of Micronesia. It can serve as a planning directory to help you choose your destination and set up your trip, as well as a reference once you're out there. An intriguing world of adventure, both land and underwater, await you in the islands.

One of the world's premier diving regions, Micronesia sprawls across some three million square miles of Pacific Ocean between Hawaii and the Philippines. With more than 2,000 islands, it covers an ocean area is as large as the continental United States, yet the total land mass would fit inside the state of Rhode Island. Some islands are little more than a patch of sand, virtually disappearing at high tide. Others are dominated by volcanic peaks and tropical rain forests. Only about 125 are inhabited.

A key to Micronesia's lure for divers is its location near the center of the Indo-Pacific realm, the richest sector of the world ocean. The closer to the center, the greater the diversity of species. If you long to see or photograph brilliant soft corals, clownfishes hiding in anemones, spectacular but deadly lionfishes, or outrageously decorated clown triggerfishes, this is the place to be. In open water you will encounter schools of snappers, jacks, batfish, and barracuda. Sharks, especially whitetips and gray reef sharks, cruise the walls at most locations. Micronesia's underwater scenery and wildlife is superb, but there's even more.

The history of World War II can be tracked across these archipelagos. Nearly every major island has historic sites, ranging from tanks and cannons and command posts on land to shipwrecks and sunken airplanes underwater. Few places in the world can match this combination of undersea wildlife, tropical island ambiance and living history. For divers the shipwrecks of Truk Lagoon, the reefs and walls of Palau, and the manta rays of Yap have become legendary. Guam, Saipan, and Pohnpei have long been major destinations for divers from Japan. And for people who want to dive off the beaten path, destinations like the Marshall Islands, Rota, and Kosrae are awaiting their discovery.

Eric Hanauer
San Diego, California
August, 2001

CHAPTER I MICRONESIA

An Overview

GEOGRAPHY

Micronesia is comprised of three archipelagos: the Marshalls to the east, the Carolines in the center and the west, and the Marianas to the northwest. There are two types of islands: high and low. The eastern sector is dominated by low coral islands with white sand beaches and palm trees, but little vertical relief. These are normally associated with atolls, which are old, mature coral reefs where the original volcanic island has sunken below sea level. The Marshall Islands are typical atolls, and some of the outer islands of Yap State (i.e. Ulithi) are atolls as well. The western Caroline Islands are primarily high, volcanic in origin, with mountains, abundant fresh water, and tropical rain forest vegetation. Pohnpei and Kosrae are prime examples. They are surrounded by two types of reefs: fringing and barrier reefs. Fringing reefs are shallow, sometimes dry at low tide, and represent an early stage in island development. Eventually a lagoon forms between the reef and the island, resulting in a barrier reef like that of Palau or Truk.

The deepest place in the ocean, the Marianas Trench near Guam, is over seven miles (11.3 km) deep. If Mount Everest were dropped into that crack, its peak would be a mile beneath the surface. Therefore the Marianas Islands may be considered the highest mountains on earth. Whether it's their proximity to the trench or just the ocean currents, the waters of Guam, Rota, Saipan, and Yap are crystal clear.

THE PAST

Humans first arrived in Micronesia 3,000 years ago, when people from southeast Asia reached the Marianas in sailing canoes. The earliest traces of civilization in the area, on Saipan, have been carbon dated to 1500 B.C. People eventually sailed westward and encountered voyagers from Melanesia, who had arrived in the Marshalls much later and headed east. These were stone-age cultures with no knowledge of metal and no written language. Yet the walls of Nan Madol and Lelu in the Eastern Carolines, the latte stones of the Marianas, and the stone money discs of Yap and Palau show evidence of complex and advanced societies with some similarities but a number of differences. Micronesians made long ocean voyages in outrigger sailing canoes, navigating by the sun, the stars, the currents, and the feel of the swells against the sides of their vessels. There are still a few old mariners in the islands who practice and teach these traditional skills.

First European contact occurred when Ferdinand Magellan reached the Marianas on his voyage around the world in 1521. By the end of the following century, Spain had occupied those islands as supply bases for their Manila galleons, which sailed between the Philippines and Mexico. Catholic missionaries arrived and converted the native people. The Spaniards were granted domain over Micronesia by the Pope, but they had minimal interest in the islands to the east because the Carolines and the Marshalls had little in the way of natural resources.

During the 19th century, traders, whalers, and Protestant missionaries from England, Germany, and the United States spread their influence through the Carolines and the Marshalls, often to the detriment of the local populace. With no immunity to the white man's diseases, death tolls were staggering. In Kosrae, for example, the population dropped from 7,000 to 300 by the late 1800's.

A clownfish, Amphiprion perideraion, peers out from its protective anemone. Five species of clownfishes are common in Micronesia.

The Spanish-American War of 1898 marked the end of Spain's empire in the region. The Philippines, Guam, and Wake Island were turned over to the United States. The remaining Marianas and the Carolines were sold to Germany, whose traders also established copra (dried coconut) and *beche de mer* (dried sea cucumber) industries in the Marshalls.

German influence ended abruptly during World War I. Japan entered on the Allied side and their fleet took Micronesia, encountering little resistance. As a reward the League of Nations granted them control over the entire region, except for Guam which remained in American hands. Although Japan's prime motivation was to establish an empire in the Pacific, its tenure in many ways was the most progressive and beneficial of all the colonial powers. They established schools, taught modern fishing and agriculture, and introduced a money economy. But as preparations for war began, their rule turned harsh. Micronesian people were forced into labor details, building airfields, harbors, and bomb shelters.

World War II made the names of Micronesia's islands household words around the world, as some of the strategic battles were fought on and over its waters, and on its shores. Guam was attacked on the same day as Pearl Harbor (December 8, because it falls west of the International Dateline) and fell in two days, giving Japan control of all Micronesia.

The United States mounted its counteroffensive in 1944. Their island-hopping campaign began by taking the Marshalls, then obliterating the Japanese fleet at Truk Lagoon, and winning the bloody battle of Peleliu. Japanese bases that weren't invaded were neutralized by heavy and repeated bombing. Guam and the Marianas were liberated in August, allowing construction of the world's busiest airfield on the tiny island of Tinian. That put Japan's cities within easy range of U.S. bombers. A year later, two of them dropped the first atomic bombs on Hiroshima and Nagasaki.

Micronesia once again became spoils of war. The entire region was turned over to the United States as the Trust Territory of the Pacific Islands. Strategists realized the importance of establishing a military presence at the eastern and western ends, and as the Cold War heated up, bases were established on Guam and Kwajalein. Nuclear bomb tests were conducted at Bikini and Enewetok in the Marshalls with little regard for native populations. Today some of those islands are still uninhabitable, and cancer rates there are among the highest in the world.

In retrospect, 40 years of American rule are cloaked in controversy. Whether by accident or design, government handouts developed a group of dependent welfare states where alcoholism, unemployment, and teenage suicide became major societal problems. Roger Emerson, an expatriate living on Kosrae stated sardonically, "We were lousy colonizers...The Japanese did a better job of developing the islands...before they turned to war. We treated it like an Indian reservation: Lock the bloody place up, don't let anybody in."

THE PRESENT

The trusteeship era ended in the 1980's and 90's as the Marshalls, the Federated States of Micronesia (FSM), and finally Palau were granted independence. Micronesia today is divided into five separate political entities. Only the Territory of Guam and the Commonwealth of the Northern Marianas (CNM, which includes Saipan, Tinian, and Rota) still belong to the United States. They elect their own governors and legislatures, their residents are U.S. citizens, but are not allowed to vote in national elections. Guam sends one non-voting member to the U.S. House of Representatives; CNM sends an observer.

The others are independent nations which have signed a Compact of Free Association with the United States. In return for subsidies (being phased out over varying lengths of time), defense and trade agreements, U.S. military ships and airplanes are allowed to use their waters, harbors, and airports.

The last trusteeship territory finally gained its independence when the Republic of Belau (usually called by its colonial name of Palau) signed its compact in 1994. It had been held up pending a conflict between its constitution, which declared Palau a nuclear-free zone, and the demands of the U.S. military which needed docking rights for nuclear ships. The conflict was decided in favor of the U.S. after several votes of the Palauan people.

The Federated States of Micronesia encompasses Chuuk (rhymes with duke) ,

Pohnpei (POWN pay), Kosrae (kosh RYE), and Yap. The names of the first three states were changed back to the original when they achieved independence. The former names— Truk, Ponape, and Kusaie —date back to German rule. It is a loose confederation, each state retaining a degree of autonomy, with the capital located on Pohnpei. The Republic of the Marshall Islands is the largest Micronesian nation, encompassing 29 atolls spread out over more than a million square miles. Outlying tribal chiefs have local authority; the seat of government is in Majuro (MA ju row).

USEFUL INFORMATION

Visitors to Micronesia will find many similarities with the United States.

Credit Cards. Major credit cards are accepted at hotels, stores, and dive centers throughout the region. Small restaurants and shops may require cash.

Cuisine. You may have to look hard to find traditional local food in Micronesia. American and Japanese cuisine prevail, although on Guam and Saipan you will find everything from McDonald's to Mexican food. Seafood lovers will be in paradise, because fresh fish is a staple of most menus. And "fresh" often means it was swimming that day. Sashimi is a special treat found throughout the islands. It's usually melt-in-your-mouth tuna, and often the cheapest item on the menu.

Coconut is the most common tropical fruit. Between dives on the islands, guides may offer you one fresh off the tree. Papaya, breadfruit, yams, and taro are other Micronesian staples, as is imported rice. In many areas people have developed a taste for canned foods like Spam, in lieu of a more natural, healthy diet.

Another American import that dominates the islands is Budweiser. Nobody can tell you the reason why, but it outsells all other beers combined. Empty cans litter the roads. Drinking isn't always done in moderation, especially in Palau, Chuuk, and the Marshalls. This triggers many a brawl on weekend nights, although aggression is nearly always directed at other locals. If you drive at night, drive defensively, because the guy in the other car may be drunk.

Currency. The U.S. dollar is the official currency throughout the region.

Dress Etiquette. Clothing is tropical informal; suits and ties are rare even in government or business. A Hawaiian-style shirt for men and a

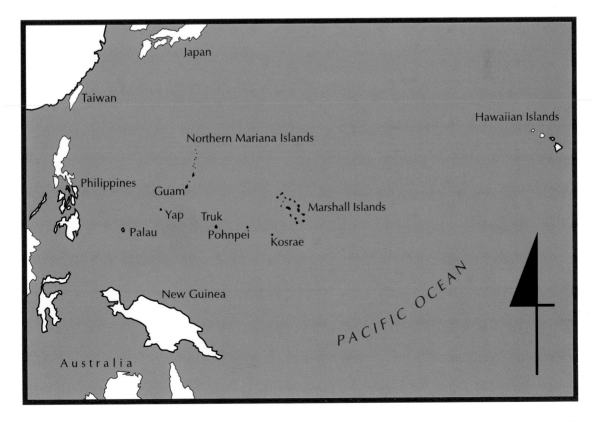

cotton dress for women pass for dress-up attire. Although women in some rural areas go bare-breasted, people are conservative and modest attire is expected. Display of women's thighs is considered offensive, so skirts or longer shorts are warranted around town, except for the big cities on Guam and Saipan. On beaches, boats, and resorts, there are no problems with short shorts or swim suits. The best advice on clothes is to travel light.

Electricity. Electricity is 110 volts, 60 cycles, and standard American plugs are used.

Getting There. Continental Micronesia, a subsidiary of Continental Airlines, is the major carrier throughout Micronesia. In the islands, it's called Air Mike. There are two ways to get there from Honolulu: direct flight to Guam or the Island Hopper. The direct flight takes seven hours, and you lose a day when crossing the Date Line between Hawaii and the Marshalls. From Guam you can catch a connecting flight to your final destination. Including a five hour flight to Honolulu from the West Coast and an airport layover, that's a long time in a plane.

The way to break it up is to ride the Island Hopper. From Hawaii to Majuro it's 4 1/2 hours, including 30 minutes on the ground at Johnston Island. That's a secured U.S. military base where chemical weapons are stored and incinerated, so transit passengers aren't allowed to leave the plane. From Majuro it's 45 minutes to Kwajalein, then an hour to Pohnpei, an hour and 10 minutes to Chuuk, then an hour and 30 minutes to Guam. At each stop the plane is on the ground about 30 minutes, and passengers are allowed to disembark to stretch their legs. One advantage of the Island Hopper is that stopovers are allowed, so it's the most economical way to see several islands.

Avoid the temptation of trying to see too much on one trip. People sometimes try to cram three or four islands into two weeks, and wind up spending an inordinate amount of time in transit and minimal time underwater. If you are in Yap only two days and the mantas aren't out in force at the time, you'll be disappointed. And if weather conditions prohibit diving Palau's Blue Corner during your four days there, you've missed out again. The major destinations, Truk, Palau, and Yap, require at least a week of diving each to do it right. On Bikini, all trips are one week. The others deserve at least three days each, and these are minimum recommendations. It's best to save the alternate destination for the next trip, and chances are you will be back because there's lots of great diving out there.

Immigration and Customs. Each state has its own immigration and customs offices, so

---

WHAT ARE YOU LOOKING FOR?

Although they have much in common, each Micronesia destination has its own unique personality. Following is a brief run-down on some of the major attractions at each island group.

Native culture: Yap, Pohnpei; **Native crafts:** Pohnpei, Palau, Marshalls; **Jungle hiking:** Pohnpei, Kosrae, Saipan, Guam, Rota; **World War II history:** Guam, Truk, Marshalls, Saipan, Palau (Peleliu); **Wreck diving:** Truk, Palau, Marshalls; **Night life & shopping:** Guam, Saipan; **Luxurious hotels:** Guam, Saipan; **Luxurious resorts:** Guam, Saipan, Palau; **Guaranteed big animal encounters:** Yap; **Live-aboard boats**: Truk, Palau; **Sandy beaches:** Palau, Marshalls, Saipan, Guam; **Novice diving:** Guam, Saipan; **Best for a non-diving companion:** Guam, Saipan, Palau, Pohnpei; **Getting away from it all:** Rota, Kosrae, Marshalls (outer atolls), Yap; **Bragging rights to friends who've been everywhere:** Rota, Kosrae, Marshalls, Tinian, Bikini.

On the verandah of his Rota Cave Museum, Matias Taisacan explains to dive operator Mark Michael how he found this Japanese anti-aircraft gun in the jungle.

A Yapese youngster's toy boat will help to prepare him for life on and around the water.

All-inclusive resorts on Saipan and Guam cater primarily to Asian tourists and their families. Activities ranging from shopping tours to tennis and diving are offered.

*A Palauan woman prepares to weave
a basket from palm fronds.*

passports are checked at the airports. This is true even when traveling between islands in the same nation. No visas are necessary for U.S. citizens, but all others will need a visa to visit Guam.

Japanese Divers. When traveling through Micronesia, especially Guam and Saipan, you might wonder who really won World War II. Japanese tourists predominate. Lately visitors from Taiwan, Hong Kong, and Korea are also coming in increasing numbers. Their importance to the region's economy cannot be underestimated. Asian tourists outnumber Americans, Australians, and Europeans by a wide margin.

Most Japanese guests in Guam and Saipan travel in groups, with the average length of stay three to five days. Their package tours are paid for in Japan, they stay in Japanese-owned hotels, and shop in Japanese-owned stores. An inordinate number of them are women in their 20's. With housing prices at home too high to save for, they have plenty of disposable income for travel.

These vacations give the Japanese a chance to do things they can't do back home. Over there, conformity and teamwork are ingrained into the culture. On vacation they can dress any way they wish, let their hair down, and forget the business suit and tie.

Over the past 20 years, scuba diving has blossomed in Japan. Like new divers everywhere, their people dream of tropical waters. Micronesia is Japan's Caribbean. It's close and inexpensive by their standards, a tropical retreat offering beaches, shopping, golf, and diving. Their gateways to Micronesia are Saipan and Guam, and an industry has sprung up to take care of them.

About 80,000 of Guam's nearly million annual visitors participate in some sort of diving experience each year. In Saipan numbers are about half that. Their experience level is similar to that of Americans in the most popular Caribbean destinations: novice.

Japanese divers are less demanding than Americans. They are used to crowded conditions, carry their own gear to and from the boat, and they follow the guide's directions with no discussion or backtalk. Their dive operations are generally more regimented than we are used to, and they tend to go to less challenging locations. Underwater, divers follow the guide in an orderly, single-file line, like ducklings behind their mother. In many places the guides feed fish, so divers are swarmed by aggressive damsels and wrasses as soon as they enter the water.

There will be occasions when the only diving available is with one of these groups. If you are able to demonstrate a higher level of competence, the guides will often allow you and a buddy to go off on your own.

Language and culture are initial barriers, but English-speaking Japanese are usually cordial and friendly if you make the first move. Many are sensitive about what they consider their poor command of English, but it's invariably better than our Japanese. Experienced divers are every bit as good as ours, especially those who travel independently. Once they have visited the Marianas a time or two with a group, they tend to venture further afield to Palau, Pohnpei, and Yap, less frequently to Truk and the Marshalls. The Japanese you meet at those destinations are more sophisticated travelers, and as skillful underwater as the best of international divers worldwide. So don't judge them all by what you see in Guam and Saipan. That's as unfair as judging American divers by what you see in Cayman and Cozumel.

Language. Forty years under U.S. Trusteeship has spread the English language throughout Micronesia. Virtually everybody in the tourist industry speaks and understands it, as well as most of the population in the major islands. Because Japanese tourism is a driving economic factor, that language is spoken extensively as well, especially in Guam, Saipan, Palau and Pohnpei. Chinese and Korean is heard in facilities catering to visitors from those countries. The Marianas have a large number of immigrant workers from the Philippines who speak Tagalog, Spanish, or English. Each island has its own native language or dialect as well.

Mail. Although some islands issue their own stamps, the U.S. Postal Service handles all the mail, and each island group has its own ZIP code. Letters sent to or from the United States require just a single domestic stamp, but delivery time can be a week or so.

Telephone. Islands have their own area codes, but there is no separate country code. To or from the US you just dial 011 for long distance, then the 3-digit area code and the 7-digit number.

Time. Micronesia covers four time zones, and the International Date Line runs between Hawaii and the Marshalls, so you lose a day when going west. Palau is 9 hours ahead of Greenwich Mean Time. At noon in Palau it's 1 P.M. in Guam, the Marianas, Yap, and Chuuk; 2 P.M. in Pohnpei and Kosrae; and 3 P.M in the Marshalls. In Honolulu it's 5 P.M. the day before, in Los Angeles it's 7 P.M., and in New York it's 10 P.M.

Tipping. Tipping is customary in major hotel and resort areas, at the rate of 10 to 15 percent. Some establishments add a service charge to the bill. Don't forget your dive guides, whether land-based or on a live-aboard. Their pay is usually low and your tip can be the difference between making it and just getting by. About ten dollars a day is a good starting point, with more for exceptional service.

Weather. Weather is tropical humid, with temperatures averaging in the 80'sF (27-32°C) year round. December through April is tradewind season, when cool winds from the northeast bring less rain and less humidity.

Abundant rainfall and a warm, humid climate nurture Micronesia's brilliant tropical flowers.

This is considered the optimum time for land travelers. But it still rains nearly every day even during the "dry" season, so pack some rain gear. During the summer, the southeast trades bring more humidity and showers. These are gentler than the winter winds, and are less likely to affect diving on the windward sides of islands. But even during the rainy season, it rarely rains all day; periods of showers alternate with periods of sunshine.

In the Atlantic they are called hurricanes, in the western Pacific they are typhoons. Both terms refer to severe storms with winds over 75 miles per hour (121 km per hr). August through December is typhoon season in Micronesia, although one may occur at any time. They usually form near the Marshalls, then gain force as they move westward. Don't be overly concerned by a typhoon report when you are in the region, because most of them miss inhabited islands and peter out at sea. Even if they hit land, major damage is rare. Guam, however, was hit by two super typhoons in the early 90's which caused severe damage.

CHAPTER II DIVING

THE ISLANDS

The dive sites in this book are arranged from west to east, beginning in Guam and continuing through the Marshalls. Each island group has certain elements, both on land and underwater, that make it unique.

Guam is Micronesia's metropolis. Catering primarily to tourists from Asia, it has luxury hotels, restaurants, and shops to supply every need. Waters on the outside reefs are exceptionally clear for diving on World War II wrecks, which are also found inside the protected harbors. If you're tired of roughing it and want a touch of pampering, but don't want to miss that diving fix, Guam is the place.

Rota, a tiny island just 40 miles (65 km) from Guam, is a return to a simpler, quieter time. With a small population and jungle-covered mountains, it's a day trip destination for Guam visitors. It also offers crystal-clear water and at least two world-class dive sites: the *Shoun Maru* and Senhanom Cave.

Saipan, a major destination of Japanese tourists, has all the comforts of the big city plus the clear water of the Northern Marianas. Its most famous dive, The Grotto, is a unique underwater experience. World War II history abounds here, both topside and underwater.

Yap, land of stone money and bare-breasted women, has become famous because of its manta rays. They gather in the channels of its barrier reef for feeding and cleaning, allowing divers close encounters with these graceful beasts. The island's outer walls offer clear water, beautiful hard corals, reef fish, and pelagic encounters.

Palau has perhaps the greatest variety of diving experiences of any place in the world. There are shallow reefs, deep walls, channels, caverns, marine lakes, current drifts, a cave, and World War II shipwrecks. As if that weren't enough, the lagoon with its incredibly beautiful Rock Islands provides a unforgetable scenery enroute to your dive destination.

Chuuk is justly famous as the home of the Ghost Fleet of Truk Lagoon. Forty-one Japanese ships were sent to the bottom during two days of intensive bombing during Operation Hailstorm in February 1944. Today the hulks are gardens of fishes and soft corals, as well as graveyards for the unfortunate crew. For American divers, this is the best known and most popular destination in Micronesia.

The high island of **Pohnpei** has long attracted visitors to its tropical rain forest, with streams and waterfalls everywhere. The best diving is in the passes through the barrier reef, where pelagics gather to take their turn at the food chain. Sharks, barracudas, manta rays, and even tunas may cruise by. When conditions permit, the offshore atolls of **Pakin** and **Ant** provide pristine walls, drop-offs, and more opportunities to dive with open-water critters.

Kosrae, a beautiful high island with mountains and rain forests, is just awakening to tourism. Kosrae is an opportunity to experience Micronesia as it was 30 years ago.

The **Marshall Islands** cover almost a million square miles (2.6 million sq km) of ocean, much of which has yet to be dived. **Majuro** and **Kwajalein** are the major jumping-off points, both offering historic wreck diving. Trips can be arranged to nearby atolls including **Mili**, **Arno**, and **Jaluit**. **Bikini** recently became accessible to divers, and its atomic test shipwrecks are a world-class attraction.

FACILITIES

Since the beginning of Micronesia tourism in the 1960's, diving has been a major draw for visitors. Some facilities and operations have a

Japanese-run dive centers, such as the Joy Dive Center on Pohnpei, usually have excellent facilities.

long track record, others are more recent, and competition is intense. Those that fall behind in service or safety quickly drop by the wayside.

Most diving is land-based; live-aboard boats are limited to Chuuk and Palau. The pros and cons of each type of accommodation are well known to serious divers. Live-aboards offer more dives per day, greater range, and convenient night diving. Land-based operations offer more spacious living quarters and a greater variety of things to do when you're not diving. This includes more opportunity to get to know the land and the people you are visiting.

On land, Micronesia has few dedicated dive resorts (defined as a hotel with an attached diving operation, where over 80 percent of the guests are divers). Perhaps the only ones meeting these criteria are the Kosrae Nautilus Resort, Carp Island Resort in Palau, and Manta Ray Bay Hotel in Yap. Many other hotels have in-house dive operations, and most dive operators will pick you up from any hotel. Among the major hotels with in-house dive operations are RRE Hotel in Majuro, Joy Hotel in Pohnpei, and Marina Hotel and Pacific Palau Pacific Resort in Palau. In Chuuk the Blue Lagoon Resort (formerly Truk Continental Hotel) serves mostly divers, and contracts with Blue Lagoon Dive Shop. Guam and Saipan have the greatest variety of hotels belonging to major U.S. and Japanese chains including Hilton, Sheraton, Hyatt, Dai-ichi, Nikko, and Pacific Islands Club. Arrangements can be made with local dive operators through the hotel or individually.

WATER TEMPERATURE

Surface temperatures throughout Micronesia range from a low of 80°F (27°C) in February to a high of 85°F (29°C) in August. An eighth-inch (3mm) wetsuit or a skinsuit will suffice for all but the most cold-blooded divers. A sleeveless neoprene vest can be added as an extra layer for night dives. Thermoclines are rarely encountered at depths less than 130 feet (39 m), and even then the temperature drop is only a few degrees.

WIND CHILL

Wind chill becomes a factor on open boats when you are wet from the previous dive. Peeling off the top of your suit will stop evaporative cooling from wind blowing over the wet nylon. A nylon or Gore-tex shell worn over your suit will reduce wind penetration and keep you warmer, even in rain.

VISIBILITY

Visibility on the outside reefs and walls typically ranges from 80 to over 100 feet (24-30+ m), with 200 feet (61 m) not unusual. Conditions inside atolls and lagoons are greatly dependent on runoff and tidal conditions. In Truk and Kwajalein 30 to 60 feet (9-18 m) is the typical range, with a constant rain of organic particles in the water column feeding the lush invertebrate life on the wrecks. The passes in Yap, Pohnpei, and the Marshalls range from a low of 20 feet (6 m) during an outgoing tide to 100 feet (30 m) when the tide is coming in. The clearest waters in Micronesia bathe the outside reefs of Guam and the Northern Marianas. Visibility is usually better in early morning before wind chop and foraging fish activity clouds the water.

WEATHER

Most of Micronesia is under the influence of the North Equatorial Current, moving warm, clear water from east to west. The southern Carolines and Marshalls are washed by the Equatorial Counter Current, flowing in the opposite direction. During the rainy season (July to December) winds are generally light and variable, except during typhoons. The powerful southwesterly winds of these storms may bring high seas up to 12 feet (3.6 m) that persist for several days.

The dry season is dominated by trade winds from the northeast, resulting in a steady northeasterly swell from three to six feet (1-2 m). This makes diving dicey on east facing sites, so activity is usually limited to the lee side of islands. During storms, the swells shift to northwest.

Diving conditions in Micronesia are generally excellent year round. Even during periods of storm swell, there is always a diveable lee area.

UNDERWATER HABITATS

In Micronesia you may be diving in a variety of different habitats: slopes and walls, reefs,

Chuuk dive operator Kimiuo Aisek named this boat in honor of 49er quarterback Joe Montana after meeting him.

channels, lagoons, harbors, marine lakes, caverns, caves, and wrecks. Strong currents are common, in fact water movement enhances the fish action at many sites. Each environment presents unique opportunities and a few problems. Working recompression chambers in Micronesia are few and far between, so responsibility for safety rests with each individual.

Slopes and Walls. The outside edges of fringing and barrier reefs may slope gradually or drop off abruptly as the sheer face of an underwater wall. When you are diving this environment, divide your attention between the colorful reef fishes and invertebrates on the wall and the schooling fishes and predators of outside water. Hard corals predominate but areas of current have colorful soft corals. Anemones may be anywhere, and many host colorful clownfishes.

Currents are a concern any time on the open ocean side of a reef, but that's where the action is. The maximum current a diver can swim against is about one and a half knots. Currents

may approach three or four knots at highest intensity, so the technique is to enjoy the ride and trust the boat to pick you up at the end. An experienced boat handler is essential, and those in Micronesia's professional dive centers are generally excellent. Pay close attention to the dive guides' briefings regarding pickup procedures. They will usually ask you to swim toward outside water, away from the reef, to be picked up by the boat. It's a good idea to bring a whistle and a safety sausage to make it easier to be noticed in big swells. Most operators don't supply them. Examples of walls in Micronesia are Ngemilis, Ngedebus, and Blue Corner in Palau, Lionfish Wall in Yap, Walung Drop-off in Kosrae, and The Crevice in Guam.

Reefs. Micronesian reefs are rich in hard coral formations, with lettuce, antler, plate, and table forms predominating. Some of the current-filled passes and walls have colorful soft corals. They aren't as prolific as those in Fiji or in the Red Sea, however the diversity of species is among the greatest in the world. The forms, shapes, and colors of the fishes are

The islands of Majuro Atoll in the Marshalls are connected by a paved road built on landfill by the U.S. Army during World War II.

Divers in Palau enjoy the breathtaking scenery of the Rock Islands on the ride out to the outer walls.

staggering, while the background is a coral fairyland. The result is a fishwatcher's dream come true.

Take care to minimize damage to the reef from inadvertent contact. Maintain good buoyancy control, so flailing movements of fins won't break off delicate hard corals. Photographers are often the worst offenders, lying down on the corals to wait for an elusive fish to come out of hiding. It isn't worth damaging a square yard of slow-growing coral to shoot one fish picture.

Channels. Channels in the barrier reefs act as funnels during tidal changes, so currents can be intense. But that's where the action is. Plankton and other organic matter are concentrated, attracting an entire food chain of fishes. Some, like manta rays, feed directly off the plankton. Others, like barracudas and sharks, eat the smaller planktivores. Some of Micronesia's most exciting dives are in channels during tidal changes.

Visibility and current are strongly dependent upon the tidal cycle. At the wrong times, visibility may be poor or the current may be too strong to hold your position. Or there may be no current at all and nothing to see. Experienced dive operators will take you into the channels at the optimum time. These are usually drift dives with live boat pickup.

Examples of these dives are Palikir Channel in Pohnpei, Goofnuw and Mil Channels in Yap, Oolong Channel in Palau, and Reiher's Pass in Mili Atoll, Marshall Islands.

Lagoons. Truk, Bikini, and Kwajalein are Micronesia's archetypal lagoons. Circulation with the open ocean is limited, so visibility is less than half that outside. These wouldn't be top dive sites without the benefit of shipwrecks. In Truk, the rain of organic matter from above keeps corals and other invertebrates well fed, and the soft corals here are as large and rich as I've ever seen. Kwajalein and Bikini are more barren, but have less marine snow. High island lagoons like Kosrae and Pohnpei have soft, silty bottoms due to extensive runoff, so diving in their lagoons is less desirable. It's important to stay off the bottom to avoid kicking up silt and ruining the already restricted visibility.

Marine Lakes. A few of Palau's Rock Islands have tiny lakes trapped within their limestone walls. There is limited circulation with the lagoon. Water seeps back and forth through the porous limestone, but the rock is a barrier to animals. Over thousands of years a confined population of fishes or invertebrates sometimes makes unique adaptations to this environment. A dramatic example is Jellyfish Lake, where *Mastigius* jellyfish in the absence of predators have lost their ability to sting. There are more marine lakes in Palau, but Jellyfish is the only one where tourists are regularly taken.

Caves. A cave is defined as a natural overhead environment where you cannot see an exit from any place within. Most submerged caves were above sea level thousands of years ago, with stalactites and stalagmites forming by water dripping through limestone. When sea level rose, the caves were flooded.

Trained cave divers use lines on long reels, and redundant lights and air supplies. If you're not cave-trained, this sort of dive should be attempted only with a professional guide who is familiar with that particular cave. There is only one true cave dive in Micronesia: Chandelier Cave in Palau. It's shallow enough to pose no decompression threat, but it's easy to get lost without a guide. Visiting divers are usually taken only into the front rooms

Caverns. If you can see the way out from any point within a natural overhead environment (as opposed to a wreck), it is considered a cavern, even though its name may end in "cave." Typically there is an opening in the top of a reef, and a vertical tunnel leading to one or more exits in deeper water. Use your air and bottom time conservatively. Begin the dive in the cavern, then take a long safety decompression stop outside. Micronesia has five outstanding cavern dives: Senhanom Cave in Rota, Blue Holes and Saies Tunnel in Palau, The Grotto in Saipan, and Blue Hole in Guam.

Shipwrecks. Micronesia is Nirvana for wreck divers. You can literally follow the course of the World War II in the Pacific by diving the wrecks from the Marshalls to Palau.

Truk Lagoon has justifiably received most of the attention of wreck divers, because its 41 ships were the result of a historic raid, which may be enjoyed as beautiful artificial reefs as well. Palau and Kwajalein are also home to sunken Japanese fleets as large and as significant as Truk, but without the rich colors of marine life. Wrecks of ships and airplanes may also be dived at Kosrae, Guam, Saipan, and Yap. Then there's Bikini, site of atomic bomb tests in the 40s and 50s, and recently opened to diving. The ships are no longer

The live-aboard Thorfinn *lies at anchor off Weno in Truk Lagoon.*

radioactive but the danger is depth, as the bottom of the lagoon is 180 feet (55 m). All of Bikini's wreck diving involves stage decompression.

Artifacts are protected by law at most sites, so look and photograph but don't take anything. Bikini's are pristine because for 50 years, only Department of Energy divers were allowed there. Truk's have been protected for many years; at other sites nearly everything was removed before the practice was stopped. There are no restrictions against handling artifacts, but 50 years underwater has rendered most of them extremely fragile. Look but don't touch is the best practice.

In some ships, the engine room skylight affords easy entry and exit, as long as divers are careful about stirring up silt. Penetration diving of the wrecks is advisable only for experienced divers with a professional guide. The dangers of getting silted out and losing your way are very real. Most of the wrecks can be fully enjoyed without going inside.

Night Diving. Warm, dry clothes and the inertia of a full stomach are the greatest obstacles to night diving. At times like that, the less hassle involved, the more likely you are to get motivated. The most convenient base for night dives is a live-aboard boat, where you can have that pre-dive snack, then go off the swim step with confidence a hot dinner will be waiting on your return.

Night dives are more difficult to arrange from land-based operations. Most of them charge extra, because there is no beach diving in front of most hotels, so boats are required to get to the dive sites. But it's worth the hassle because night dives here can be dramatically different. In the shallow waters, lobsters, crinoids and sea urchins come out of hiding in the shallows. At intermediate depth you will find sleeping fishes, crabs, octopuses, and perhaps feeding morays. In open water you may see the blinking eye pouches of flashlight fish, as their bioluminescent bacteria mimic miniature automobile headlights.

MARINE LIFE DIVERSITY

The diversity of Micronesia's marine life is staggering. Over 200 species of hard and soft corals can be found in Yap alone. The entire Carribbean has only 67 species. Palau has an estimated 1,357 inshore fish species, with the Marshalls and the Marianas tapering to 827 and 872 respectively. By comparison, Hawaii has only 460 species.

POTENTIALLY DANGEROUS CREATURES

Humans aren't normal prey for marine animals, not even sharks. Rarely will a creature act aggressively toward us, because we are among the largest and ugliest things in the ocean. However every successful organism has survival strategies. For us, it's brain power. Marine animals use speed, size and strength, teeth, armor, camouflage, or venom to eat and to keep from being eaten. Sometimes despite our superior intelligence, we blunder into situations that place an animal into a fight or flight situation. It's then that we risk injury.

Urchins. The most dangerous animal in the sea, in terms of numbers of injuries to divers, is the sea urchin. Tropical urchins like those found in Micronesia are nocturnal; they remain holed up during the day. But at night, be careful where you kneel or place your hand, because it may be on one of these spiny critters. The most common is *Diadema*, with long, slender, and extremely sharp spines. On contact, you will feel an initial sharp sting, as the tip of the brittle spine penetrates your suit and your skin, then breaks off.

As soon as possible, try to pull the spine straight out, with tweezers if available. If part of the spine breaks off in your skin, try to remove it as you would a splinter, using a needle that has been sterilized with alcohol. Sometimes soaking the affected part in vinegar helps, because the acetic acid may dissolve the calcium carbonate spine.

Jellyfish. Unless you develop extreme sensitivity, most jellyfish stings are merely irritating, with effects disappearing within less than an hour. If you do get stung, be careful not to rub it, because each tentacle contains thousands of stinging cells called nematocysts, that act like miniature hypodermic needles. Parts of transparent tentacles often tear off and remain on your skin. If you rub or scratch, any nematocysts that haven't already fired will discharge their load of venom into your skin. External application of ammonia or alcohol will neutralize jellyfish venom.

People who have had previous adverse reactions to jellyfish stings could go into anaphylactic shock as a result of a subsequent sting. Among the symptoms are inflammation, fever, and restricted breathing. If this happens, monitor the victim's breathing and give rescue breathing if needed. This is a life-threatening emergency, so get medical attention as soon as possible.

Fire Coral. Fire coral (*Millepora*) is found in most of the world's tropical seas. Not a true coral, *Millepora* is a hydroid with a yellowish calcareous skeleton. Close inspection will reveal tiny hairs that contain nematocysts, which do the damage. When brushing against fire coral you will feel an immediate stinging, burning sensation. The severity of symptoms depends upon the victim's sensitivity to the toxin. Sometimes a rash will develop that can itch periodically for several weeks after initial exposure. Neither jellyfish nor fire coral can sting through protective suits, so wearing those and gloves will prevent contact with the nematocysts. If you do get stung, immediate application of meat tenderizer will often relieve all symptoms. Mix the powder with water to make a paste, and put it directly on the sting. Enzymes in the meat tenderizer break down the proteins in the venom to neutralize its effect.

Crown of Thorns Starfish. Crown of thorns are a natural predator of corals and in some places around the world constitute a threat to the health of a coral reef if their numbers reach plague densities. This has not been the case in Micronesia. A major predator is the Triton's trumpet snail, and in areas where this shell is collected, crown of thorns populations have increased. This starfish's twenty-armed bodies are covered with sharp spines that can penetrate a glove, and their mucus is slightly venomous, enough to feel a sting. The pain usually disappears after a few minutes.

Moray Eels. Moray eels are common throughout the islands, but are dangerous only when mishandled. There are more than 50 species of morays in Micronesia. These are usually gentle animals that are afraid of divers, but they do have sharp teeth which they use to defend themselves when cornered. Their eyesight is also notoriously poor, and of the few bites that occur, most are while hand feeding. A finger may be mistaken for a tiny fish.

Sea Snakes. Despite venom more deadly than a cobra, the sea snake is a shy, retiring animal that presents a hazard only if grossly mishandled. Small snakes with alternating black and white bands, sea snakes have tiny fangs that can barely go through a wet suit. They aren't common, but can sometimes be seen on land or in air pockets in caves as well as underwater. Bites of humans are so rare as to be practically unheard of, primarily because the snakes try to avoid human contact. Divers are sometimes photographed handling them, but that's not prudent because of their heavy artillery.

A moray eel, Gymnothorax javanicus, *peers out from a coral crevice.*

Venomous Fishes. Among the venomous fishes of Micronesia are the stonefish, scorpionfish and lionfish. All have hollow spines on the dorsal fin or on the pectorals or cheeks that can penetrate suits and skin, and inject venom. The most dangerous is the stonefish, an elaborately camouflaged creature that looks like a part of a rock or reef.

Stonefishes are not very common, and their nearly perfect camouflage renders them virtually invisible. Most people who claim to have seen one were probably looking at a scorpionfish. The true stonefish lives in coral crevices in shallow sandy areas, and looks like a rock with a frown; its downturned mouth and the tiny eyes are key characteristics.

The most venomous fish in the world, wounds from stonefish spines are extremely painful and have been known to result in death. Fortunately, they are not aggressive toward people. Be careful when walking over reefs—shuffle your feet, and wear boots with substantial soles. Scorpionfishes are also camouflage experts, preferring to hide motionless in holes or under corals to ambush prey. At night they sometimes lie in the open on the reef. The spines on the dorsal and pectoral fins are venomous, causing swelling and severe pain. A diver would almost have to lean on one to get stung, because they don't move very much. If you do get stung, immerse the injury in water as hot as you can stand. Heat denatures the protein venom. Compared with stonefish, scorpionfishes have large, prominent eyes and a more typical fish mouth.

An old saying among divers is, "If it's ugly, don't touch it". The lionfish is an exception to the rule, because it is one of the most beautiful fish in the sea. It is also one of the most venomous, the sting causing excruciating pain

Tufts of algae enhance the natural camouflage of this venomous scorpionfish, Scorpaenopsis sp. *They are very difficult to spot and they usually lie motionless in holes and under coral to ambush their prey.*

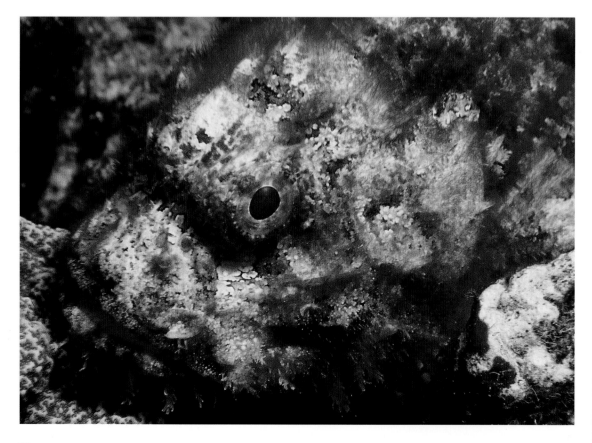

and even some fatalities. There are six species in Micronesia. *Pterois volitans* is sometimes called the zebrafish, turkeyfish or firefish. The enlarged pectoral fins look like wings. These fish often swim slowly just off the bottom and, when threatened, usually turn their back, pointing their venomous fins at the enemy. They are well aware of their heavy artillery, displaying a calm demeanor around divers and hovering as if they owned the place.

Sharks. Sharks are common at many Micronesia locations, to the point of almost taking them for granted. Whitetips are the most common on the reefs, most in the four to five foot (1.2-1.5 m) range. They are often seen resting on sand bottoms, usually in the channels. Next in terms of numbers are gray reef sharks: powerful, full-bodied sharks that are reputed to be dangerous. They like currents, often patrolling water outside a wall,

usually maintaining at least 20 feet (6 m) of personal water space between themselves and divers. At times they may be actively hunting fishes, swimming purposefully and darting quickly at their prey. Then it's best to maintain a low profile and remain near the wall. Blacktips are slightly less common, with hammerheads limited to the Carolines and Marianas. Silvertips, oceanic whitetips, and tiger sharks are among the big guys that roam the area, but sightings of these animals by divers are rare.

In all my dives in Micronesia, I've never seen a shark act threatening in any way. On the contrary, typical shark behavior is swimming away when a diver approaches. If you get close to a shark, consider it a privilege. Shark feeding shows haven't made it yet to this part of the world, so their behavior is about as natural as can be in a region with a lot of divers.

Lionfishes, Pterois volitans, *armed with venomous spines, are common in Micronesia. They are easy to approach, but avoid sudden movements that could make them feel threatened.*

CHAPTER **III** GUAM

AT A GLANCE

Guam isn't a world renowned glamour destination like Truk, Palau, or Yap. Yet because it is Continental Micronesia's international hub, trips to those exotic destinations usually begin and end there. It's the commercial center of Micronesia, with facilities, shopping, and infrastructure that you won't find anywhere else in the islands. It's got some interesting diving, a variety of activities on land, and good people who will do their utmost to help out a visiting diver. Guam can serve as a place to overcome jet lag and check out your skills and equipment before heading to the prime destination. Or it can provide a rest and re-outfitting break between destinations on a longer trip.

If you need supplies like film or dive booties at reasonable prices, this is the place to get them. Guam has full-service dive shops where equipment and parts, including some hard to get items, are available at prices no higher than stateside. It's a freeport, where shipping costs are relatively cheap, and competition helps keep prices down. If you crave a touch of luxury after roughing it in Kosrae, Guam has it. And you can take advantage of the island's good diving, or hop over to Rota or Saipan which are a half hour away by air.

Although tourism is now Guam's number one industry, visitors prior to 1962 needed a permit to disembark because it was a U.S. military reservation. Pan Am initiated direct flights from Japan in the late 1960's, and that started far eastern tourism. Today Continental Micronesia is the region's major air carrier.

Tourism is not only responsible for the island's economy, but also its infrastructure. Developers and the government built the roads and facilities to serve visitors and to get workers to and from the hotels.

Japanese have little vacation time, so a trip to Guam becomes four to six days of freedom. They are in the same time zone, and flights are only three to four hours duration. Among Guam's attractions are easy accessibility, safety, and a favorable exchange rate. Word of mouth from returning tourists has promoted a favorable image. Numbers of visitors from Hong Kong, Korea, and Taiwan are steadily increasing as well.

The initial impression of Guam is dominated by Tumon Bay's Hotel Row, operated by and for vacationers on their first trip to America. That's right. Guam is so far west, it is the United States' easternmost territory. It's the home of two major military bases, their strategic value upgraded since the closing of bases in the Philippines. It's got familiar fast-food and commercial chains that make it seem like home: from McDonalds and Sizzler to Ben Franklin and Safeway. Tamuning (ta MOON ing) and Tumon (TOO mon) Bay seem like one big shopping mall.

Micronesia's largest land mass at thirty two miles long and four to eight miles (6.5-13 km) wide, the island is divided into two halves. About 70 percent of the population is in the northern half, which has most of the development, including the University of Guam, the airport, a military base, and Hotel Row with its attendant shopping district. The southern half is rain forest, rural villages, and a more relaxed, laid-back lifestyle. In the interior are mountains, jungle, rivers, and waterfalls.

Chamorros (cha MOR rows) are the indigenous peoples of Guam, having sailed from the Malay region of Southeast Asia some 3,000 years ago. They had a thriving culture

Its deck gun is long gone, but the gun platform of the Tokai Maru *forms a dramatic natural frame for a hovering diver.*

centered around the sea. Their homes were thatched and woven, set atop foundations of latte (LA tay) stone which still can be seen in some locations around the island. These consisted of a limestone pillar up to 20 feet (6 m) high, and a capstone. Some date back over 1500 years, all the more remarkable because the ancients had no metal tools for quarrying.

Most Chamorros have Spanish surnames, which were assigned for the purpose of record keeping during Spain's colonization of the islands. Today they are in the minority, representing only 43 percent of the population. Filipinos, Caucasians, Japanese, Korean, Chinese, Indians, and Pacific Islanders have emigrated to Guam, making the island a cosmopolitan community of various customs and traditions. But the Chamorro language is still taught in schools to keep it from dying out. Their greeting, "haf adai" (pronounced "half a day" and meaning, "How are you, how's it going?"), is the official motto of Guam.

WEATHER

During the dry season, January through April, the northeast tradewinds are the strongest. From late March through August the tradewinds taper off,there is maximum sun and very little wind. August is usually the quietest month for sea conditions. The rainy season runs from mid July through November. Typically the sun shines in the morning and rain falls in theafternoon.

Typhoons are possible from August through November, but some of the worst ones have been in May. They don't often hit Guam, but when they do the effects can be severe.

THINGS TO DO ON LAND

The best way to get around on Guam is to rent a car. Although roads aren't marked as clearly as they could be, people are always willing to help. Route 1 is the main road along the northern coast, so you can always orient to it. The south provides a peaceful escape from city life, and can be seen on a one-day drive. Among the sights are the remains of a 200-year-old Spanish fort, World War II bunkers and artillery pieces, jungle waterfalls, and beautiful beaches.

Guam was one of only three United States territories to be occupied by a foreign country. (The other two were tiny islands in the

Aleutians, all taken by the Japanese early in World War II.) To commemorate the 50th anniversary of the liberation (July 21-August 11, 1944), War in the **Pacific National Park** was dedicated in 1994. A beautiful memorial in the Nimitz Hill area overlooks Asan Bay and the invasion beaches, offering breathtaking views of the harbor. On a clear day you can see Rota, some 47 miles (76 km) away. Carved bas relief tablets atop the hill depict events of the war years, while maps, charts, and pictures trace the progress of the U.S. invasion. A small museum on the beach displays the story of the war in detail. Operated by the National Park Service, it has exhibits, pictures, newspaper stories, and photographs that make the war come alive.

Although the bright light district is **Tumon Bay**, **Agana** (a GAN ya) is the island capital. It is the oldest western city in the Pacific, founded in 1668. All that's left of the pre-war town is **Plaza de España**, the governor's gardens. Some old buildings actually survived

This memorial at War in the Pacific National Park commemorates the liberation of Guam by American troops in 1944.

Tumon Bay is Guam's bright light district, featuring luxury hotels, fine restaurants, and shopping.

the war, but the U.S. military thought the town needed rebuilding and tore them down. Agana today is a quiet residential city where the locals go to shop and eat. It also houses a small historical museum and a 160-foot (50 m) public swimming pool for those who like their exercise in fresh water. Agana is the home of the Pacific Daily News, Micronesia's most influential newspaper.

If fine dining and night life is your pleasure, Tumon Bay has it all. There are over 30 hotels with more than 7,000 rooms, and over 250 restaurants. The large hotels are definitely upscale, but some bargains are available on package prices through travel agencies. Restaurants run the gamut from Japanese to steak houses, Italian to seafood, Mexican to fast food. There are night clubs and bars, shooting ranges and jewelry stores, and shops of all kinds. Even if you aren't staying in one of the big hotels on the bay, try to stop there for an evening dinner or drink, and enjoy the view.

DIVING

Guam welcomes over a million tourists a year. Sixty to eighty thousand of them participate in some sort of dive activity, ranging from introductory dives to certification and trips. Most local dive operators cater primarily to novices from Asia taking advantage of low-priced group packages. Many visitors come to Guam to learn to dive, and do it in a three-day period. Some have done their pool work and academics in Japan and come here to do their open water dives.

Local operators suggest that if people are going to dive here, they should do it before visiting Truk, Palau, or Yap. Most tourist diving takes place in and around **Apra Harbor**, where sites are available in any weather conditions. Visibility inside doesn't match the crystal-clear outer waters, but there are interesting reefs and some historic shipwrecks.

A tourist submarine, the **Atlantis**, rated to 150 feet (45 m), takes non-diving visitors to the reefs inside the harbor. Its visit makes for an interesting diversion while diving the reefs. Two larger surface subs with glass walls (actually glass-bottom boats on steroids) also ply the harbor reefs. On the surface, there are jet skis, parasailers, snorkeling boats, and harbor cruisers. Everybody is on the water, so there is lots of work for boat skippers.

On a per capita basis, Guam has one of the most active diving communities in the world. Out of 125,000 residents, approximately 2,000 to 3,000 are divers. The numbers fluctuate because military personnel are often transferred, but any way you cut it, that's a big percentage. About 7,000 people on Guam are certified annually through PADI USA. This even includes a few Japanese, who consider an American certification a status symbol.

For an American tourist, going diving in Guam is almost like going diving in California or Florida. You visit a dive shop and book a trip on a charter boat. Most of the large boats cater to groups of Japanese, but there are a few smaller ones that serve local divers, at local prices. By working through shops catering to locals, a visiting diver can meet buddies, rent equipment, and arrange boat trips. The major

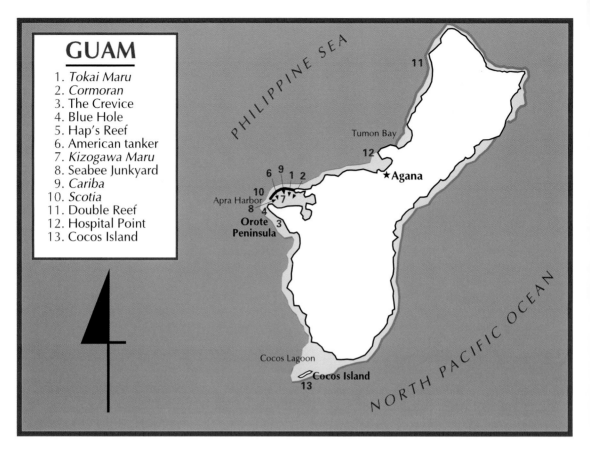

GUAM

1. *Tokai Maru*
2. *Cormoran*
3. The Crevice
4. Blue Hole
5. Hap's Reef
6. American tanker
7. *Kizogawa Maru*
8. Seabee Junkyard
9. *Cariba*
10. *Scotia*
11. Double Reef
12. Hospital Point
13. Cocos Island

PHILIPPINE SEA

NORTH PACIFIC OCEAN

Tumon Bay

Agana

Apra Harbor

Orote
Peninsula

Cocos Lagoon

Cocos Island

store on Guam is Micronesia Divers' Association (MDA). It's a friendly place to shop, to get acquainted with local divers, or just to get some current news about other Micronesian destinations. They can usually set you up on a day boat with 24 hours advance notice. If you walk in that morning, you would probably be placed on a larger boat with a group of beginners. Boats leave at 9 A.M. and return about 2:30 in the afternoon, because by 4 o'clock the visitors have to be on the bus for their shopping tour.

DIVE SITES

Most charter boats run out of Agat (A gut) Bay or Apra Harbor, carrying 16 to 35 people. Among the popular destinations are Blue Hole and The Crevice, spots that get major coverage in Japan.

Perhaps Guam's most unique dive is inside Apra Harbor where wrecks from two world wars lie intertwined. The *Cormoran* was a German gunboat that was interred in the neutral harbor at the beginning of World War I. When the United States entered the war in 1917, the harbormaster ordered the surrender

of the ship. To prevent it falling into enemy hands, the German captain set off an explosion which sent it to the bottom. The *Tokai Maru* was sunk by an American submarine some 25 years later, during the attack on Guam. The wrecks of two world wars and two nations now lie across each other on the bottom of the harbor.

1. *TOKAI MARU*

DEPTH:	40-125 FEET
	(12-38 M)
LEVEL:	INTERMEDIATE TO
	ADVANCED

This 440-foot (133 m) freighter was sunk in 1943 by an American submarine. It lies at a 45° incline on its port side, resting against the *Cormoran*. Depths range from 40 to 125 feet (12-38 m); the best depth to see most of it is 80 feet (24 m). There are five holds, with torpedo damage in number four.

This is a more photogenic wreck than the *Cormoran*. Black and orange rope sponges run along the rail and the bow, which was mangled by the bombs. Lots of gears and machinery remain on the deck. Immediately behind the bow deck is a beautiful gun turret, but the gun is long gone. Dramatic silhouettes can be achieved from underneath. The wheelhouse is topped by a large smokestack, the wreck's most dramatic feature. There is also an H-mast canted at an angle. Gears and winches are strewn about the deck, with not much marine growth.

2. CORMORAN

DEPTH:	80-125 FEET
	(24-38 M)
LEVEL:	INTERMEDIATE TO
	ADVANCED

The *Cormoran*, 334 feet (101 m) long and 46 feet (14 m) wide, was a Russian mail ship, built in 1909, and captured by Germany in 1914. Three years later, on the day the U.S. declared war on Germany, it was scuttled by its captain. Seven crewmen died in the explosion that sank it in four minutes.

The ship lies on its starboard side, below the middle of the *Tokai Maru*. To find it, just swim over the side of the *Tokai* about midships. There is also a marker chain leading directly to the *Cormoran*. Depth to the deck is 80 feet (24 m), to the bottom 125 feet (38 m), but most of the wreck can be seen without going deeper than 100 feet (30 m). It is usually silty, with visibility in the 30-foot range, but occasionally opens to 100 feet (30 m) on an incoming tide.

Penetration diving of this wreck is not recommended; people have died in the attempt. It is safe, however, for experienced divers to enter the engine room, because the exit can easily be seen. But stay off the bottom to avoid silting. A "promenade deck" provides another interesting photo spot. The 90° orientation lends a surreal feeling to this dive. Don't waste time looking for artifacts; the

The wreck of the World War I German ship, Cormoran, *lies underneath the Japanese freighter* Tokai Maru, *from World War II.*

Mary Radcliffe-Gicca views a giant sea fan at the floor of The Crevice, 150 feet (45 m) beneath the surface.

Cormoran has long since been picked over, and what's left is protected by law.

These wrecks are seldom visited by charters, because most Japanese don't like diving war wrecks from their country. But they often dive a nearby American tanker, which is little more than a cement water barge.

3. THE CREVICE

DEPTH:	60-150 FEET (18-45 M)
LEVEL:	INTERMEDIATE TO ADVANCED

Visibility on Guam's outer walls is usually in excess of 100 feet (30 m). When conditions permit, one of the most popular dives is The Crevice. It's often used by instructors as an introduction to deep water diving because the water is usually so clear you can see your boat from the bottom. The mooring buoy is attached to a large Navy anchor atop the reef at 60 feet (18 m). A classic kedge about 15 feet (5 m) long, it was moved here from another site.

The crevice is a u-shaped crack in the reef with sheer walls beginning at 80 feet (24 m), then dropping vertically to a 160-foot (50 m) bottom. A huge boulder, 30 feet (9 m) around, fills the base of the crevice. A cascading stack of sea fans on the outside edge of the boulder is a prime spot for photographers. Surgeonfishes and bannerfish hang around the sea fans, and an occasional school of barracuda may be seen as well.

4. BLUE HOLE

DEPTH:	60-130 FEET
	(18-39 M)
LEVEL:	ADVANCED

One of Guam's premier sites, this dive can be made only in calm seas, because the location is right against a rocky cliff. Boats can't anchor there in a big swell. The Blue Hole is a vertical shaft in a fringing reef, beginning at 60 feet (18 m) and dropping to about 300 (91 m). At 120 feet (36 m) is an opening to the outer wall. This is obviously an advanced dive, requiring careful planning and an experienced guide.

A natural limestone cavern, Blue Hole is entered through a wide fissure in the reef top at 60 feet (18 m). Inside are a few beautiful sea fans, but for the most part the walls are barren. A large window opens to the ocean at 120 feet (36 m), where prudent divers make their exit, because the hole continues well past sport diving limits. Many divers just drop to about 100 feet (30 m) to look around, then return through the opening on top. Gliding downward in a slow-motion freefall, the vertical shaft seems very wide, so there is no claustrophobic feeling.

Sea whips begin around 90 feet (27 m), and the best concentration of sea fans is around the window. This is a good dive for photographers, with potential for interesting wide-angle setups.

5. HAP'S REEF

DEPTH:	25-60 FEET
	(8-18 M)
LEVEL:	NOVICE TO
	INTERMEDIATE
ACCESS:	BOAT

This shallow, flat-topped reef is one of the best places on Guam for observing and photographing reef fishes. It's a volcanic formation almost as long and wide as a football field, with more marine life in one area than any other place in Guam. Fishes have been fed by divemasters over the years, so they aren't in the least bit shy. Resident groups of lionfishes hang out along the reef walls. After dark, the nocturnal creatures take over, including moray eels, Spanish dancers and other nudibranchs, and tiger cowries.

For the most part, fishermen leave the reef alone in deference to dive tourism, but there have been instances of spearfishing and even dynamiting in the past. However, the reef has healed itself and now offers easy, benign marine life encounters for divers of all levels.

OTHER DIVES OF NOTE

When seas are rough, diving is limited to the vast expanse of Apra Harbor. Visibility inside ranges from 30 to 60 feet (9-18 m). In addition to the *Cormoran* and the *Tokai Maru*, there is the "**American tanker**" (6), the ***Kizogawa Maru*** (7), and the **Seabee Junkyard** (8), a collection of halftracks, bulldozers, and pieces of the ocean liner ***Cariba*** (9). Several reefs inside the harbor are visited by tourist submarines, where feeding stations have been set up to attract fishes. The critters are used to divers and not at all skittish, so these are good areas for close-up photography. Outside the breakwater is the wreck of the ***Scotia*** (10), a steamship that sank in 1907 Although not intact, it's pretty and clean, and because it's outside, visibility is usually in excess of 100 feet (30 m).

When weather permits, an excellent dive on the northwest side of the island is **Double Reef** (11). Schools of spinner dolphins sometimes hang out there, or may be spotted on the way. The reefs surround sand pits in shallow water, and have beautiful hard coral formations. **Hospital Point (12)**, off Tamuning, is a pretty wall dive with lots of big sea fans.

Off the southernmost tip of Guam is **Cocos Island (13)**, wreck site of a 17th century Spanish galleon. Professional salvors have brought up a fortune in gold and silver coins, and continue to work the site. Unfortunately, it's off limits to sport divers.

CHAPTER IV NORTHERN MARIANAS

AT A GLANCE

The Commonwealth of the Northern Marianas encompasses 14 islands extending some 400 miles (645 km) from Rota in the south to Farallon de Pajeros in the north. Only the southernmost three—Rota, Tinian, and Saipan—accommodate tourists.

As a commonwealth, these islands have a closer political association with the United States than any other Micronesian destination with the exception of Guam, which is a U.S. territory. Residents are U.S. citizens and carry U.S. passports. The Commonwealth is self-governing, but foreign affairs and defense are under Washington's jurisdiction.

The 11 northern islands are mostly uninhabited, with a total population under a hundred. Some are active volcanic zones; five have experienced eruptions in this century. Saipan is the most intensely developed island, with a heavy annual influx of Japanese tourists. Among Micronesian destinations, it ranks second only to Guam in that department. Rota is an exceptionally beautiful high island that hasn't yet been scarred by excessive development. Tinian, best known as home base for World War II atomic bombers, is mostly ranch land.

One characteristic all the islands share is incredibly clear water. Located along the Marianas Trench, the deepest part of the world ocean, and washed by the waters of the North Equatorial Current, visibility of 200 feet (61 m) is not unusual.

For divers heading to Palau or Yap via Guam, a side trip to Rota offers a chance to get acclimated to the area and critters, in addition to a couple of outstanding dive sites. Saipan also has wartime wreckage underwater, as well as some good reef sites. If you happen to be there on a business trip, diving opportunities abound. As for Tinian, access is difficult and there is very little infrastructure for visiting divers.

WEATHER

The rainy season is July through October, with the warmest temperatures in June. Average monthly rainfall during that time is 10 to 15 inches (26-39 cm), but precipitation usually just passes through, leaving many sunny hours during the day. The northeast trade winds blow from November through March; the wind is usually from the east May through October. Typhoons can occur any time, but are most likely between August and December. No more than one will hit an island in a normal year. Air temperatures are in the 80'sF (27-32°C) and low 90'sF (33-34°C) year round, with high humidity. Water temperatures are always in the low 80'sF (27-28°C), so skin suits will do the job for all but the most sensitive divers.

Rough seas are most likely in January and February. Visibility drops below 100 feet (30 m) only during storms and the fall typhoon season. Most dive sites are located in East Bay, within a 10-minute boat ride from the dock. If conditions are too rough on one side of the bay, diving is always available on the other side.

ROTA

Located just 54 miles (87 km) northwest of Guam, Rota is an overlooked gem that is usually ignored by divers headed for the big name destinations. A beautiful island with

The engine of a Japanese bomber lies in 30 feet (9 m) of water in Siapan's Tanapag Harbor. It exploded on contact, scattering wreckage over a wide area.

Dive guide Jon Pearlman aims a Japanese cannon that once guarded Rota's East Harbor.

mountains, jungle, spacious parks and beaches, it is a quiet, natural retreat from the bright lights and the concrete high-rises of Guam and Saipan. For divers it offers arguably the clearest water in Micronesia, along with at least two world-class dive sites: the *Shoun Maru* and Senhanom Cave.

The Marianas are part of a submerged mountain range, rising more than 36,000 feet (10,909 m) from the floor of the Marianas Trench. Above water, the island is what Guam must have been like 35 years ago. It lacks some of the luxuries, but has comfortable places to stay, good food, friendly people, and some excellent diving.

Rota is served by Northwest Airlines. Flying time from Guam or Saipan is thirty minutes.

THINGS TO DO ON LAND

Rota's major landmark is **Wedding Cake Mountain**, so named because it resembles a layered wedding cake. Along its flanks and on top of the opposite plateau is lush, verdant jungle. Monitor lizards, fruit bats, and coconut crabs may be encountered along the dirt roads and footpaths, with wild orchids growing along the sides. A stream runs down to the ocean in a series of small waterfalls. To the south is a **bird sanctuary**, with a pathway and stairs where you can stand atop a cliff and watch the birds soar above and beneath. Terns, red-tailed tropic birds, boobies, kingfishers, and others fly overhead, while in the jungle below are nests of red-footed boobies.

The land atop the mountain is public and available to any Rota citizen for farming. (Most hire Filipinos to do the farming for them.) The road is a rutted dual track, with the underbrush in the middle as tall as the hood of a truck, so four wheel drive is recommended. At land's end is a microwave tower with incredible views of Songsong Village and Wedding Cake Mountain.

The population of Rota consists of about 1,500 Chamorros and an almost equal number of foreign workers, mostly from the Philippines. The major event of the year is the **Rota Fiesta** in October, honoring the island's patron saint, San Francisco de Borja. Parties are everywhere, their success measured by the number of tables of food. Local fare has a Spanish flavor, featuring red rice, plantain, taro, bananas, seafood, and roast whole pigs. Visitors are always welcomed.

The busiest time for tourism is May. Golden Week, a major Japanese holiday, brings tourists from there, while Americans come in from Guam and Saipan during Memorial Day weekend. The slowest time is November.

Although Rota saw no land combat during World War II, the island was a Japanese military base. In a hillside bunker overlooking Wedding Cake Mountain and East Harbor is a Japanese cannon. It is about 25 feet (8 m) long, and so finely balanced that one person can turn it through about a 150° arc. The only problem is that the locals decided to improve on history with a camouflage paint job in pastels: pink, gray, and light blue.

In the **Rota Cave Museum**, island history has been collected and put on display. It is the project of Matias Taisacan, a native who was raised in Columbus, Ohio and returned home to pursue his hobby of collecting antiques. Hacking his way through the jungle, he has found artifacts ranging from ancient Chamorro taro grinders dating back to A.D. 1100, to guns, ammunition, and bombs from World War II. They are displayed in a cave on the family property, which Mat has transformed into a museum. It's well worth the admission charge especially if Mat is there to guide you.

Another manifestation of Rota's heritage is the **Latte Stone Quarry**. These mysterious structures, consisting of a pillar topped with a mushroom-shaped cap, were used as foundations for homes. They are found in Guam, Saipan, Tinian and Rota. Nobody knows how they were quarried, since iron wasn't available to the native people at the time. Now overgrown by the jungle, some of the stones still lie in the ground, as if waiting for someone to raise them for their intended purpose.

There are two upscale hotels, the **Rota Hotel** and the **Rota Resort and Country Club**, with the island's first golf course that opened in 1995. Although they welcome the money, people are still ambivalent about development. After all, Songsong Village's main road wasn't paved until 1992, and there still are no traffic signals.

Rota radiates a friendly ambiance. People wave at each other on the road, supposedly because most of them are related, but they wave at visitors as well. It's quiet and unspoiled, yet has the current day's newspaper, cable television, and stores where you can buy most things. There is an aura of middle class prosperity that isn't present on many other islands in Micronesia. It's green and beautiful and the diving, although a step below Truk, Palau, and Yap, is still very good. This Pacific paradise is a true gem.

DIVING

Intermediate and advanced qualifications are necessary to take advantage of the best diving on Rota. Most of it is deeper than 60 feet (18 m), and some is in overhead environments, although daylight can always be seen.

Big animals are occasional visitors. Dolphins may come in during spring or fall. March to May is fishing season for mahi-mahi and marlins, which have been spotted underwater in late spring and early summer. During fall, turtles will emerge to lay eggs on the island.

Dive Rota, owned by Mark and Lynne Michael, is the operation Americans and expats usually dive with. They provide transportation from hotel to their shop, located near the dock.

Virtually all the known dive sites are located on the southeastern end of the island. There is a lot of area still unexplored, so even more interesting sites may soon be available to adventurous divers.

The ancient Chamorros quarried these latte stones (shafts) and capstones without the use of metal implements. They were used for foundations of royal buildings in Guam and the Marianas.

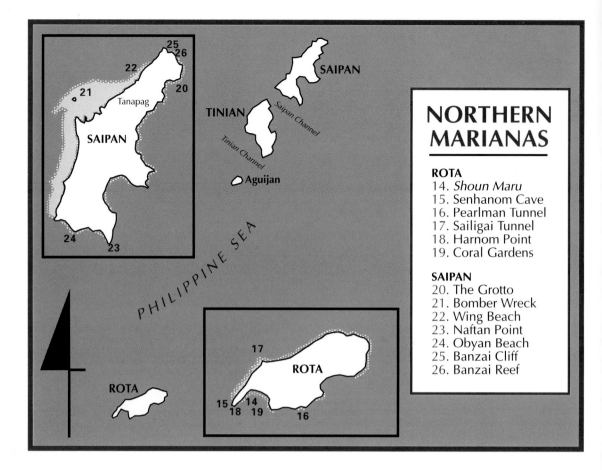

NORTHERN MARIANAS

ROTA
14. *Shoun Maru*
15. Senhanom Cave
16. Pearlman Tunnel
17. Sailigai Tunnel
18. Harnom Point
19. Coral Gardens

SAIPAN
20. The Grotto
21. Bomber Wreck
22. Wing Beach
23. Naftan Point
24. Obyan Beach
25. Banzai Cliff
26. Banzai Reef

DIVE SITES

14. *SHOUN MARU*

DEPTH:	DECK:
	70 FEET (21 M)
	HOLDS:
	85 FEET (26 M)
	SAND:
	110 FEET (33 M)
LEVEL:	INTERMEDIATE TO
	ADVANCED

For underwater photographers, the *Shoun* (Shawn) *Maru*, a 393-foot (119 m) freighter is a dream come true. Because most shipwrecks are found in waters of limited visibility, one of the most difficult things to depict is the overall look and feel of the vessel. On this one you can drop back and shoot the broad vistas, depicting its massive size and bulk.

She was sunk in July 1944, hit amidships by a single torpedo dropped from an American fighter plane, and went down within three minutes. No crew was aboard at the time. The ship rests upright in the sand at a depth of 110 feet (33 m), and from the surface one can see

The Shoun Maru*'s giant steam engine was exposed during a salvage attempt in the 1960's. The 200-foot (61 m) visibility is typical of Rota.*

almost its entire length. The bow and stern are virtually intact, towering over the mangled central section of the ship. In the late 1960's, a local resident did some salvage work, using dynamite to access the middle.

Being able to see and photograph the massive boilers and the triple expansion engine is one of the unique features of this dive. On most wrecks, the engine is hidden deep within the bowels of the ship. Because the salvage attempt exposed the midships area, all mechanical parts are out in the open.

In the forward hold are two trucks, one upright and intact that provides an excellent photo spot, especially if you can squeeze in front of it and shoot back out. A pair of motorcycles are near the stern. Numerous artifacts spread about the wreckage include a tiled bathtub, lanterns, saki bottles, cups, cartridges, and guns.

One thing lacking on the *Shoun Maru* is extensive marine life. Because the clear waters are fairly sterile, this wreck lacks the colorful soft corals and encrusting organisms found in Truk Lagoon. But this has helped maintain its integrity as a classic shipwreck.

The site is about a 10-minute boat ride from the dock, and is protected from all but direct south swells. Therefore it can be dived virtually any day. The only caution is its depth since most of the wreckage lies at 80 to 90 feet (24-27 m). This is a square profile dive, so if you are using a computer, be conservative.

15. SENHANOM CAVE

DEPTH:	40-80 FEET
	(12-24 M)
LEVEL:	NOVICE TO
	ADVANCED

Senhanom Cave is an underwater grotto with a dramatic archway entrance at a depth of 40

A WW II Japanese truck lies in the forward hold of the Shoun Maru.

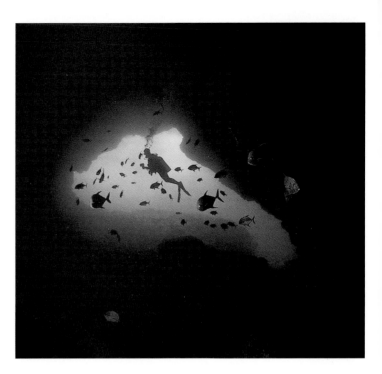

A school of jacks inside the side entrance to Senhanom Cave.

feet (12 m), and an inner chamber illuminated by an overhead skylight. The excellent visibility allows dramatic silhouettes when the sun is streaming through the skylight. Because of low overall light levels, photographers will need slow shutter speeds and fast film .

Although a light is needed to view details on the walls and in darker corners, the exit can be seen at all times, making this a safe, shallow dive. Whitetip sharks may be encountered as they swim through the cavern. Groupers, squirrelfishes, and jacks are common residents, as are lobsters hiding in the crevices. The long white antennae of the lobsters make them look much larger than they really are. Four different types of cowries are found inside, but shell collecting is forbidden. A side exit is decorated with delicate sponges and lace corals, along with a spectacular flame scallop that sports a vivid electric bolt pattern outlining its lips. This exit also makes for dramatic silhouettes.

The reef flat in front of the cave is a breeding ground for horse conches; hundreds lie scattered throughout the area. A series of crevices runs throughout the reef, housing lobsters, morays, and whitetip sharks. The drop-off then continues to 150 feet (45 m). Pelagic visitors spotted here include tunas and marlins. Along the wall, divers have reported big Napoleon wrasses, sharks, and tuna chasing baitfish.

16. PEARLMAN TUNNEL

DEPTH:	50-80 FEET (15-24 M)
LEVEL:	INTERMEDIATE TO ADVANCED

Named after a former Dive Rota guide, Pearlman Tunnel is a large overhang that actually consists of several tunnels or crevices going back into the reef. Some are tight squeezes, and your tank may scrape on the ceiling as you squirm inside. Squirrelfish and hatchetfish mill about in the darkness. Ledges inside are filled with lobsters that are extremely shy. Their color is predominantly black, decorated with orange spots, but the first thing you will notice are their long white antennae.

Outside the tunnel are lots of reef fish including butterflies, angels, parrotfishes, anthias, and an occasional clown trigger along the predominantly gray bottom, decorated with occasional sea whips and fans. Common marine life also includes lionfish, Napoleon wrasses, morays, and stingrays in sandy areas.

Depth outside the cavern ranges from 50 feet (15 m) down to the lower edge of the reef at about 80 (24m). The current usually runs west, so divers drift along the reefs. Located on the east side of the island, access to this site is dependent upon weather and surf conditions.

17. SAILIGAI TUNNEL

DEPTH:	45-90 FEET
	(14-27 M)
LEVEL:	INTERMEDIATE TO
	ADVANCED

Sailigai Tunnel (SAL i guy) resembles a lava tube. From above, it is just a hole in a gray reef. Entry is usually from the deep end, 70 feet (21 m), swimming uphill and exiting through the reef top at 45 feet (14 m). But by starting shallow and heading downhill, it's like a fairyland, exiting from the gray tube into brilliant blue water. The tunnel is wide enough for two divers to swim side by side, but it's best to go slowly and single file to avoid damaging some of the delicate lace corals, sponges, and sea fans that line the walls.

The reef itself slopes down to about 90 feet (27 m). There are anemones with several species of clownfish. Lionfish hover around crevices, schools of black triggerfish and rainbow runners hang out in the waters above, along with occasional tuna. This is a great spot for viewing sharks, especially when there is a current. Whitetips and blacktips are common, along with an occasional gray reef shark. Nurse sharks sometimes hide under ledges. During late spring and early summer, whitetips are sometimes seen mating.

At the northern end where the reef meets the sand is an arch formation resembling a desert bridge. To the south is a crevice shared by lobsters and lionfish.

18. HARNOM POINT

DEPTH:	50-160 FEET
	(15-50 M)
LEVEL:	ADVANCED

Beginning at 50 feet (15 m), the profile is like a staircase paved with big boulders, eventually continuing into the deep ocean. Scenery is dominated by these huge rocks; there is very little growth on them.

At 100 feet (30 m) is a natural cul de sac. Composed of more rocks, it is called the Fishbowl, and houses angels, butterflies, basslets, and Moorish idols. Protected from the current, divers can remain in the Fishbowl and watch the pelagics outside. Jacks and sharks often cruise in closely; they seem to be getting used to divers. A variety of open water fish is always on display, including red snappers, jacks, tunas, Napoleon wrasses, sharks, and barracudas. Large oceanic whitetips have also been spotted here on occasion, as well as turtles. Because of the depth and unpredictable currents, this is rated the most difficult dive on Rota.

19. CORAL GARDENS

DEPTH:	20-90 FEET
	(6-27 M)
LEVELS:	NOVICE TO
	ADVANCED

Perhaps the easiest dive is Coral Gardens, a protected area with sand channels in the reef at depths ranging from 20 to 60 feet (6-18 m). The unusual coral formations and colorful reef fish are the highlights of this site. There are clownfish colonies, occasional sharks, and Napoleon wrasses. At one time the fish here were spooky because of spearfishing, but now they have become used to divers and are friendlier.

Nearby are the remains of two Japanese submarine chasers. The most intact one is at 90 feet (27 m), surrounded by a garden eel colony. The engine, shaft and propeller, smokestack, depth charges, machine gun, anchor chain, and signal lamp can still be identified. This was originally thought to be a fishing boat, and the depth charges were supposed to be 50-gallon (19 dkl) drums. Mark Michael of Dive Rota took extensive measurements and videos and showed them to the park service, who matched the numbers with their records and confirmed the true identities. They also warned divers not to touch the depth charges. The same caution goes for bullets that can still be found on the site. Mark picked one up and it went off in his hand. He recalled, "I didn't feel anything, pulled my fingers out of the cloud, and still had them all. I'm glad it was a bullet and not a depth charge. I hate to see people scraping and tapping those things."

TINIAN

Tinian's main claim to fame is that the **Enola Gay** took off from there to drop the first atomic bomb on Hiroshima, 1,700 miles (2742 km) away, on August 6, 1945. Three days later another B-29 from the same airfield bombed Nagasaki, which brought an abrupt end to World War II. At that time Tinian's airfield was the busiest in the world, as U.S. bombers used it to attack the Japanese mainland. Today the two runways are deserted and overgrown with weeds. Simple signs and plaques mark the site of the pits where the atomic bombs were stored.

The island is shaped something like Manhattan, so homesick soldiers named the roads of the base Broadway, 42nd Street, and 8th Avenue. Today most of the island is a cattle ranch, with only one town, **San Jose**, and a population of about 1,000. There are two small hotels and one dive operation, all catering to Japanese. Dive sites on the island are still being explored and established. Among them are North Point, a dumping ground for World War II wreckage, Nilho Point, where blacktip and whitetip sharks hang out, and Jimmy's Point, an underwater grotto.

The distance across the channel to Saipan is three miles, and Saipan dive operators make infrequent trips to Tinian when weather conditions permit. It is easier for them to dive the established sites on their home island, and the beginning divers they cater to prefer shorter rides. It would be difficult for an individual tourist to find out exactly when they are headed to Tinian.

With its clear water, low population pressure, and rocky coastline, Tinian shows promise of some excellent diving. But infrastructure and access will have to improve for that promise to become reality.

SAIPAN

Saipan has come full circle. Once the site of a Japanese wartime stronghold, the island today is a stronghold of tourism, with close to a half million visitors a year, about 80 percent of them from Japan. Additionally, the numbers of visitors from Taiwan, Korea, and Hong Kong are steadily increasing. **Beach Road** in **Garapan** is the main drag, with block after block of high-rise hotels, restaurants, and shops, with signs in Japanese.

Saipan isn't a place where experienced divers would go as a prime destination. But if you are there on a business trip or have some layover days on a diving vacation, this is a place where you can get into warm, clear water and see things of interest, ranging from World War II wrecks to marine life to unusual topography.

During the waning days of World War II, the runways of Tinian were the busiest in the world. The Enola Gay *took off from here to drop the first atomic bomb on Hiroshima.*

THINGS TO DO ON LAND

The island offers a wide range of comfortable hotels and tourist facilities. Businesses catering to Japanese tend to be pricey, but like anywhere, bargains are available if you go where the locals go. Bright light districts are centered around the major hotels. If shopping and night life is your interest, Saipan's is among the best in Micronesia. There are wall to wall gift shops featuring American items like towels with dollar bill designs, Disney characters, and sports logos. Other businesses feature name brand and designer apparel, golf equipment, and of course Karaoke bars. Seductively dressed hostesses attempt to entice pedestrians into their bars, while restaurants and non-franchised fast food places of all descriptions round out the neighborhood. At **Nino's Pizza**, for example, dinner is an eclectic cultural mix, with Chamorros baking Italian-American pizza for Japanese diners.

Hotel Row and its attendant shops occupy only a small area; the rest of the island is still green and unspoiled. Many visitors never look beyond the glitz, but there are some beautiful spots on the wooded northern part, as well as historic **World War II sites**. In the interior are jeep trails, a jungle cave system, and an old **Japanese airfield** complete with guns and tanks. Safari tours on four-wheel-drive vehicles can be arranged through local agencies. Compared to Guam, Saipan is quieter and more laid-back, but still has the comforts and bright lights of a big city when you want them.

During World War II, Saipan was a strategic Japanese base. When the invasion came on June 15, 1944, civilians by the hundreds committed suicide by jumping off two northern cliffs, because they were told that American troops would commit atrocities. United States invasion forces used loudspeakers and leaflets urging them not to jump, assuring that they wouldn't lose face or be harmed. Parents pushed their children off, then followed to their death. Witnesses report that Japanese soldiers prodded, pushed, and threatened to shoot those who didn't go voluntarily. Over 30,000 Japanese civilians and military personnel perished before the battle was declared over on July 9.

Today there are shrines on both cliffs. **Banzai Cliff** overlooks the ocean and the surf breaking on the rugged northern coastline. The white terns circling below are said to be carrying the souls of the dead. Ironically, this is also the location of one of Saipan's best dive sites.

Suicide Cliff is nearby, but further inland. A sheer rock formation covered with dense jungle foliage, its green tranquillity belies its violent history. A shrine is located on top of the cliff, and at its base are the remains of cannons and a tank. Their bright camouflage paint job seems incongruous with war relics at other places, where a patina of rust lends a sense of history.

The **Last Command Post** is a fortified cave near Suicide Cliff, surrounded by the rusted remains of tanks and machine guns. It is said that General Saito, when he realized defeat was imminent, committed hara kiri here by plunging a dagger into his stomach.

The remains of a **Japanese prison** in the woods were rumored to have held Amelia Earhart after her ill-fated flight. That lady got around (see Mili Atoll in the Marshalls, page 114).

Along the western coast of the island are several miles of white sand beaches, all open to the public despite their location in front of hotels. A fringing reef protects the beach from ocean waves, forming a natural harbor of sorts. There are dozens of stands where locals rent beach accessories ranging from umbrellas and surf mats to kayaks, windsurfers, and jet skis. Parasailing and water skiing are also available.

Many of the hotels are all-inclusive resorts, where the price covers all meals and activities. They also offer rooms only, for a lower cost. One such establishment is **Pacific Islands Club**, a large hotel built around a freeform, multi-level swimming pool which has water slides, a swim-up bar, and even a pirate ship for kids to play on.

DIVING

There are some excellent dive sites in Saipan, but access may be difficult. The skippers and guides are obligated to their major customers: tour groups consisting mostly of beginners. The vacationers do a lot of partying at night, some get seasick, and they don't like to go into rough water. If you have a group of about six people, it may be possible to get on a separate boat. Individuals may be able to hook up with an operator who isn't tied up with tour groups.

Meeting a longtime need of advanced

divers, Rick Northen recently opened **Stingray Divers**, a full-time professional store which caters primarily to locals, expatriates, and visiting Americans. He offers all services including instruction, sales, rentals and trips. Like MDA in Guam, this is a place for visiting Americans to go diving.

DIVE SITES

20. THE GROTTO

DEPTH:	50-80 FEET
	(15-24 M)
LEVELS:	INTERMEDIATE TO
	ADVANCED
ACCESS:	WALKING

A limestone sinkhole opening to the sea, The Grotto is Saipan's best known dive. A concrete stairway of 109 steps leads down from the parking lot to a large pool of water underneath a cantilevered half dome of rock, overgrown by jungle. The pool surges in response to the wave action outside; the water is a deep, transparent blue. The entry is a jump off a large boulder at the edge of the pool.

Underneath is a huge, dark cave, illuminated by a misty blue light filtering from above and from three subterranean openings leading to the sea. Sponges and delicate lace corals are attached to the walls. Large rock formations and tumbled boulders line the horizontal slots to the ocean, which offer dramatic silhouettes for photographers. You can swim through any one of the three slots at 50 feet (15 m) to the reef outside. Instantly you are surrounded by schools of small fish, dominated by sergeant majors who obviously have been well fed by previous divers. A crevice in the reef is filled with beautiful yellow gorgonians and sea fans. Sharks, tunas, and eagle rays may be seen swimming along the wall. Sixty feet (18 m) above, the surf breaks violently against the cliff.

Caution. The entry-exit slots may be hard to spot from outside. If you cannot find your way back inside the grotto, there is no way to exit the water along the sheer cliffs. So if you aren't

with a competent local guide, don't stray too far from the holes. Make sure you re-enter the cave with enough air for a safety stop inside.

In a driving rain, The Grotto becomes even more eerie and dramatic. The stairs become a waterfall of brown, muddy water cascading downward, carrying rocks and gravel with it. A tan cloud the color of *cafe au lait* spreads out over the blue surface of the pool. You drop down quickly to keep the cloud behind you during the dive. Afterward you ascend back into the muck, which by now has diffused over the upper 25 feet (8 m), barely allowing you to see your instruments. The safety stop and final ascent is like diving in chocolate milk.

The only drawback of this unique experience is slogging back up the stairs with full gear. But that's a minor price to pay for a memorable dive.

21. BOMBER WRECK

DEPTH:	30 FEET
	(9 M)
LEVEL:	NOVICE TO
	ADVANCED

One of Saipan's most dramatic dives is at a depth of only 30 feet (9 m): the Bomber Wreck in Tanapag Harbor. Japanese divers are told that this is the wreck of a B-29; to Americans it is a Bouncing Betty, a Japanese seaplane set up as a bomber. There are pieces of a radio with Japanese writing on it, which seems to establish the origin. Also, the turret gun has a flared barrel, which is supposed to be a feature of Japanese artillery. The plane exploded in the air and wreckage is strewn about a 50-yard (45 m) area.

The Grotto, a sinkhole with an exit to the ocean, is Saipan's most renowned dive site.

Ben Concepcion hovers over the gun turret of a Japanese bomber in Tanapag Harbor, Saipan.

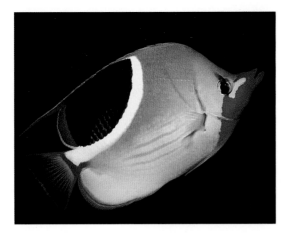

Many fishes change color at night. Above is the saddled butterflyfish, Chaetodon ephippium, *during the day. Below is the same species at night.*

A huge, four-engine bomber, the wings are almost intact, imparting a feeling of size and scale. But it is the engines and their four-blade propellers, broken away from the wings, that convey the sense of power. There is no recognizable fuselage. What's left of the instrument panel lies inside a twisted aluminum structure, very small and badly damaged.

Besides the engines, the most dramatic feature of the wreck is the upper ball turret. It is almost intact, made of sheet aluminum, with a gun protruding at a 45° angle. The gunner must have been scrunched up in a ball to fit inside, not an assignment for six-footers (2 m) or claustrophobics of any size.

Most of the wreckage is covered with algae, despite lots of herbivorous fish swimming around. Sergeant majors are everywhere,

obviously used to being fed. Because of the shallow depth, clear water, and reflective white sand, this is a dramatic photo spot.

Located not far away from the bomber are a Japanese transport ship, a submarine chaser, several landing craft, and a Japanese minisub. All are in 35 feet (11 m) of water or less. A local guide is needed to find them.

22. WING BEACH

DEPTH:	30-80 FEET
	(9-24 M)
LEVEL:	NOVICE TO
	ADVANCED

The fringing coral reef has two interesting formations: a crevice dropping from 50 to about 75 feet (9-23 m), and a coral arch decorated with colorful invertebrates. Among the interesting reef fishes are birdnose wrasses, groupers, and boxfishes. Cleaner wrasses are out in force, picking parasites off larger fish. Look in tiny holes within the reef for mantis shrimp. In the crevice, look for lionfishes and squirrelfishes.

Butterflyfishes, especially pyramid butterflies, swarm about like bees, a bit too frantically because they expect food from the dive guides. Some of the large yellow-eyed snappers are unusually tame, also due to feeding.

Caution. This dive may also be made from the beach, but because of surf and currents, this should only be attempted by advanced divers familiar with the area.

23. NAFTAN POINT

DEPTH:	40-115 FEET
	(12-35 M)
LEVEL:	NOVICE TO
	ADVANCED

Naftan is the southernmost point of Saipan. It's a sloping wall with sand channels in the top of the reef at about 40 feet (12 m). This dive begins among beautiful hard corals, then heads to a deep wall that leads into the Saipan-Tinian channel. Snappers, triggers, groupers, and small wrasses swim around the wall, which becomes more vertical near the end, with sharks and Napoleon wrasses cruising the area. When there is a strong current, look to outside water for barracudas, gray reef sharks, eagle rays, or tunas swimming by. The pelagics make this site exciting. When there is no current, the outside action is tame, so divers must turn their attention to reef life.

When sea conditions permit, boats go around the corner to Forbidden Island, on the eastern side of the point. It's actually a peninsula, an island only at high tide, and great spot to camp. Locals catch lobsters on the reef in 10 feet (3 m) of water. It's called "Forbidden" because the Chamorros think evil spirits live there. People have been washed off the rocks by waves.

Because this site is difficult to get to, there is low diving pressure. The best area is from 40 to 50 feet (12-15 m). The structure is a sloping wall with finger reefs, covered by staghorn and table corals. When there is a current, this is also a good spot for pelagics.

24. OBYAN BEACH

DEPTH:	30-60 FEET
	(9-18 M)
LEVEL:	NOVICE TO
	ADVANCED
ACCESS:	BEACH

Easy access, shallow water, beautiful corals, and consistently good visibility make this a popular beginners' dive. It's possible to enjoy this without going deeper than 40 feet(12 m). Eels, lionfish, clownfishes, and shrimp inhabit the reef.

Intermediate and advanced divers can swim to the outer reef at 55 feet (17 m) to look for larger fish, including Napoleon wrasses and eagle rays. Whitetip sharks rest in sandy crevices. On the way out, look for a colony of garden eels in the sand at 40 feet (12 m). Occasional rip currents can make exit difficult, but a rope is there to assist.

25. BANZAI CLIFF

DEPTH:	40-70 FEET
	(12-21 M)
LEVEL:	NOVICE TO
	ADVANCED
ACCESS:	BOAT OR BEACH

This dive can be done May through August, when the cliff is in the lee of prevailing winds. Even then it's surgy, so beginners should opt for boat access. Follow the cliff line from north to south and avoid the temptation to go deep. At the beginning, you will descend and enter the first of two caves, bordered with colorful coral formations.

The second cave is the reason to make this dive. A skylight allows sunshine to spill in from overhead, illuminating the interior which is home to lobsters, lionfish, and octopuses. Exiting the cave, swim south along the cliff to the site where the Japanese committed suicide in 1944. The U.S. military dumped machinery off this cliff after the war, and the area is strewn with tank tracks, propellers, wheels, bullets, and artillery shells. Some of the ammunition is still alive, so look but don't touch.

26. BANZAI REEF

DEPTH:	40-80 FEET
	(12-24 M)
LEVEL:	INTERMEDIATE TO
	ADVANCED

This site is perpendicular to Banzai Cliff and begins where the previous one ended. You will swim through an arch at 50 feet (15 m) and follow the wall into the ocean. It has numerous holes and small caves with occasional moray eels and lionfish. At the end of the reef are schools of tunas and barracudas, as well as occasional eagle rays.

Caution. Be careful of currents as you come up above the wall. On top of the reef, the current usually runs from north to south.

CHAPTER **V** YAP

AT A GLANCE

Fifteen years ago, few people had heard of Yap. Today it joins Palau and Truk as one of Micronesia's Big Three, a must-see destination for divers. It has become renowned for opportunities to get up close and personal with manta rays. But Yap is more than mantas. Outside the fringing coral reef are pristine walls with 150 foot (45 m) visibility. These jungle islands are home to the most traditional society in Micronesia, where women go bare breasted and giant stone disks are used for money. It's a peaceful retreat to a time gone by, a chance to see Micronesia as it was before war and high-density tourism changed it forever.

Because of conditions unique to Yap, the movements of the mantas have become so predictable that divers are able to go out during favorable tides and observe them feeding on plankton and being cleaned. Nobody, guest or guide, is allowed to interfere with the mantas in any way. Consequently, divers are treated to a unique opportunity to observe one of the ocean's most graceful creatures in a wild and natural state.

Yap has preserved its heritage to the greatest degree of any Micronesian state. Many other islands have succumbed to the heavy influence of both western and Asian culture. Time doesn't stand still for any people, but Yap has resisted many of the influences of modern society. The easy pace of life is a throwback to the days when these western Caroline islands were considered an earthly paradise.

Part of the reason is its location off the beaten tourist path, lying between Guam and Palau. Over half the state's annual visitors are divers. The locals consider this low-impact tourism, because after a day on and under the water, divers are usually too tired to go out carousing at night.

Yap is part of the Federated States of Micronesia, along with Truk, Pohnpei, and Kosrae. Yap proper, which includes the capitol town of Colonia (population about 1,000), consists of four islands connected by bridges and surrounded by a barrier reef. There are an additional 14 outlying atolls, but none is open to tourism. The local name for the islands is Wa'ab, but it became Yap to the rest of the world when the first Europeans reached its shores in the 16th century. The foreign captain pointed toward the island and asked its name. Thinking he was pointing at his canoe paddle, the native chief answered, "Yap." The story may be apocryphal, but explains as well as any why the state is known to the rest of the world as "canoe paddle."

There are only 60 miles (97 km) of road on Yap proper; fewer than 20 of them are paved. Women in the villages still go bare breasted, wearing only a wrap-around skirt called a *lava-lava*. In town, most of them wear dresses or T-shirts. Although they have no qualms about breasts, decorum dictates keeping the thighs covered, and that goes for visitors as well. Women tourists are advised to wear knee-length dresses around town. Many men wear loin cloths, although western attire is usually worn in town.

Wooden houses with corrugated tin roofs are the most common form of dwelling. Everything is overgrown with jungle foliage; outrageous wildflowers line the roadway. Although the standard of living cannot compare with industrialized nations, many families own cars, and people seem happy and well fed.

Yap is known as the Island of Stone Money. Carved disks of crystalline limestone can be found along the roadside, next to ceremonial meeting houses, or in jungle clearings called

When mantas pass directly overhead divers are awed by their majestic size.

stone money banks. These disks, called *rai* (rye), range from two to twelve feet (.6-3.6 m) in diameter, and were shaped with primitive tools like clam shells and stone. A hole in the center allowed them to be carried on a wooden pole. Nobody knows how long ago the Yapese began making them, but old fragments have been carbon dated to A.D. 125 Many were destroyed during the Japanese occupation, others taken away for souvenirs. Fewer than 7,000 *rai* remain.

Each one has a name and a specific owner, although it may be located far from his home. Its value is determined not by size, but by history. All stone money was carved from a special type of crystalline limestone, quarried on certain Rock Islands of Palau, then transported by canoe across 250 miles (403 km) of open ocean to Yap, a five day journey. Pieces that came over on particularly hazardous trips, where canoes and men were lost, have greater value. By the late 19th century, Yapese artisans began shaping the stones with metal tools. An American trader, David (His Majesty) O'Keefe, transported them from Palau via sailing ship. These later stones, although smoother and more finished looking, have less value than the older ones. With the coming of the 20th century, the practice of making stone money ended. It is used today to pay societal debts such as wedding dowries or reparations for insult and injury, but also can serve as collateral for monetary loans.

In town, most people make their living working for the government. In the villages, the men fish while the women tend the taro patches, cook and take care of the children. The women work harder growing yams, bananas, squash, pumpkins and green beans than the men do fishing.

The centerpiece of each village is the *faluw*, or men's house. These structures, made from native materials with thatched roofs, are always built on the site of a former men's house. They are used for village meetings, bachelors' quarters, and for male puberty rites. The only native women allowed inside are servants or concubines. A few *faluws* are open to tourists of both sexes.

The concept of private property is paramount in Yapese culture. It's a small state and land is precious. All land off the roads is owned by somebody, and etiquette requires asking permission before walking across their turf.

The children of Maa Village perform folk dances to keep traditions alive. All proceeds for scholarships.

WEATHER

November through May is tradewind season, blowing from the northeast. Diving during that period is done mainly on the lee side. May through October is the rainy season, with showers usually in the afternoon. Air temperatures average in the low 80'sF (27-28° C) year round. Yap is south of the major typhoon belt, but may be hit on occasion.

THINGS TO DO ON LAND

Colonia is a quiet village that goes to sleep early. But there is no dearth of things for visitors to see and do on Yap if they are interested in nature and culture.

A hike up **Medeqdeq** (Med DEK dek) **Hill** provides a breathtaking view of Colonia and the bay. Although less than 500 feet (152 m) high, the heat and humidity can make it seem higher. Be sure to admire the wildflowers.

On Saturdays, the children of **Maa Village**

put on a **cultural show**, performing traditional dances in ornate costumes, depicting the history of their people. This serves the purpose of keeping traditions alive and raising money for scholarships. Visitors can sample local foods and watch native crafts being made.

Although Yap was not involved in land battles during World War II, the remains of a Japanese airfield lie next to the present airport. The wreckage of **Zero fighter planes**, strafed on the ground, is still there to see, along with rusting anti-aircraft guns.

On the northern end of **Maap Island**, the village of **Bechiyal** (BESH ee al) is set up as a cultural center. It has one of the oldest *faluws* in Yap, now serving as a museum. With prior arrangement, it is possible to stay there overnight with a local family, or to camp in the men's house.

The oldest *faluw* open to visitors is in the village of **Okau**. An ancient pathway, paved in stone and coral blocks, leads there through the jungle. On the way, you will pass taro patches with vast colonial spider webs, and mud flats with colorful red crabs. Thirty-six pieces of stone money are arrayed outside the men's house. The biggest of the disks, seven feet (2.1 m) across, is blackened by years of jungle growth. Okau is a cool, peaceful refuge.

The village of **Rull** (rool) is about a mile (1.6 km) hike from Manta Ray Bay. At the municipal office, the roadway is lined with about 30 pieces of stone money. Follow the dirt road to the right to a men's house by the bay, bordered by more stone money. The nearby traditional village of **Balabat** is surrounded by taro patches, jungle foliage, and wildflowers.

Yapese people don't like photographs taken of their houses or everyday tasks. They know from videos and catalogs how westerners live, and feel somehow you are demeaning them by shooting photos of women cooking over an open fire or of people living simply. Ask

Men's houses (faluws) are used for meetings, bachelors' quarters, and male puberty rites. The limestone disks surrounding the structure are rai, the stone money that has become the icon of Yap.

Betel Nut

People throughout the western Pacific chew betel (beetle) nut, and the most potent is said to come from the palm trees on Yap. It's supposed to provide about a 10-minute high, something on the order of tobacco but without the noxious chemicals. It stains teeth red, eventually turns them black, but is said to prevent cavities.

Beetle nut paraphernalia is carried in a pouch made of banana leaves (or a Ziploc bag for non-traditionalists) containing the nuts, pepper leaves, and a salt shaker full of coral lime. Men and women alike carry these "purses" everywhere.

In the interest of research, I tried some. After splitting the nut by biting down, I wrapped it in a piece of pepper leaf for flavor, sprinkled it with lime to stimulate saliva flow, then popped it into my mouth and began to chew. The texture was like a piece of manila rope and almost made me gag. My spit came out bright red, as if someone had socked me in the mouth. Other than that I didn't feel a thing, and after 5 minutes, spit out the wad. Definitely an acquired taste.

permission before shooting people pictures.

Along the roads are middens of aluminum cans carrying the Budweiser label. For unknown reasons, Bud has become the preferred beverage of Micronesia, and empty cans litter the roads like red, white, and blue weeds. A thousand years from now, when archaeologists dig through the remains of these islands and come across these non-biodegradeable artifacts, what will their conclusions be?

Yapese handicrafts don't compare with the ones available in the Marshalls, Pohnpei, or Palau. But some stores sell green glass fishing floats, which are picked up by old men along the beaches. They are authentic, some even have an embossed Japanese seal. They are sold strung with macramé nets of coconut fiber.

Bill Acker

The man whose promotional flair put Yap on the diving map is Bill Acker, a personable, down-to-earth Texan who came as a Peace Corps volunteer in 1976. Assigned to introduce modern business methods to Yap, he

eventually became general manager of Waab Transportation, the state's major employer. They operate cargo docks, own construction, insurance, and cement businesses, and are the region's Budweiser distributor. Bill convinced Waab that diving tourism had a future in Yap, so they built the Manta Ray Bay Hotel in 1989. Four years later he bought it, along with the dive operation, and now runs both full time.

Acker combines American business sense with respect for Yap's culture and for the underwater environment. The island has cast its spell on him as well. Bill built his dream house on a secluded beach on the island of Maap, where he lives with his Yapese wife, Patricia, and their four children. He is responsible for the strict rules that prohibit interfering with manta rays.

Diving with Mantas

In a way Acker has become a victim of his own success, because the diving world associates Yap exclusively with manta rays. Actually, this would be a prime diving destination even without the mantas, because the outer reefs

Seen from the top of Medeqdeq Hill, the town of Colonia has only 1,000 inhabitants, yet it is the capitol and the most populous place in Yap.

PHOTOGRAPHING MANTA RAYS

The essential rule is to be patient and let the rays come to you. If you swim toward one, you may get off a quick shot, but the animal usually swims away. If you remain close to the bottom, some will continually circle your position. At times they will pass within a snorkel length, so a Nikonos 15mm lens is ideal.

Find a rock or coral head in their path, away from large groups of divers. Get upcurrent so that they will be facing you to feed, wrap your legs around a rock for stability, and wait.

Take a meter reading from the section of the water column you wish to use as a background. Then power down the strobe to compensate for the high reflectivity of the ray's white underside. For example, at a 4-foot (1.2 m) distance at 5.6, I normally use 1/4 power and bracket by backing up the strobe, first 4 feet (1.2 m), then 5 feet (1.5 m) or more. A kiss of light will bring out detail on the manta's underside; a blast will result in a white glare.

Because of the plankton in the water column, hold the strobe far off camera to minimize backscatter. Hand-holding the strobe allows quicker reaction to the fast moving mantas.

The best way to get close to mantas is to hug the bottom and let them pass directly overhead.

offer pristine hard corals, prolific and varied marine life, and excellent visibility. But because manta rays are the dominant image of Yap, any description of its diving must begin with them.

A fortuitous combination of geography and weather patterns allows diving with mantas (*Manta birostris*) year round. The western Pacific around Yap is plankton poor, as evidenced by its generally excellent visibility. This factor tends to keep the rays near the island. Two major passes through the fringing reef drain the lagoon, concentrating and funneling available plankton where the channels become narrow and shallow. The animals move regularly into these channels—one on the east side and one on the west—for feeding and cleaning,

Tradewinds blow from November to May, making the west side of the reef (Mil Channel) diveable. From June through October, the best diving is on the eastern side (Goofnuw [pronounced gawf'new] Channel). These dives are tide dependent; mantas move in during tidal changes. Therefore departure times for divers are variable; it is best to arrive at slack high tide. On one day the manta dive may depart at 8 A.M.; on another it may leave at 1 P.M. If high tide occurs in the middle of the night, manta diving is on temporary hold.

There are several other channels in Yap's fringing reef, and mantas have been seen in all of them. But their movements are predictable only in Mil and Goofnuw, so manta dives are planned for those locations.

While chances of seeing mantas are better on Yap than virtually anywhere else, these are still wild animals and nothing is guaranteed.

Everything is dependent on tide conditions, time of year, and perhaps just the chance of being there at the right time.

Bill Acker and dive guides Jesse Faimaw and Leo Ragman have arguably more first-hand experience with manta rays than anybody in the world. They have dived with them almost daily for a decade, and the following are some of their insights and observations.

Ideal time for manta diving is one hour before high tide. At the last of the incoming tide, plankton-carrying currents are slack enough for divers to maintain position without being swept away. As the tide begins to turn, plankton is funneled out of the mangrove areas and the mantas become really active. When high tide occurs in the morning there are more of them around, so if your first day of diving in Yap has high tide at 8 A.M., you might be able to dive mantas every day of your stay.

Mid-tide is the mantas' prime environment. At that time they hover very happily, with tons and tons of water bringing them food. But the current is too much for most divers. If the mantas are flapping their wings even slowly, you can bet there is a raging current.

On days when you hit it right, Mil Channel can be pristine with visibility in the 100-foot (30 m) range. The rays gather at a 25-foot (8 m) ledge called Manta Ridge. Despite poorer visibility, Goofnuw Channel has some advantages. Mantas are spread out over five distinct cleaning stations, so divers can get away from one another in small groups. Also, many whitetip sharks hang out on the sandy bottom of the channel.

The best time to dive mantas is between 9 and 11 in the morning. At that time there is about a 95 percent chance of seeing them. Late in the afternoon, you may strike out.

When there are lots of divers, it is best to sit still and remain where the guide puts you. It doesn't matter how many people there are as long as everybody stays down and no one chases the mantas. They'll take a look at the divers, then do whatever they want to do. Strobes don't bother them; it's when photographers move above the coral heads to get closer that the mantas move away. So the most important thing is to remain still and be patient; there is a better chance they may come to you. As they pass overhead, hold your breath momentarily or exhale slowly. Most of them don't like bubbles.

The key is to look in all directions. Leo invariably spots them about 10 to 15 seconds before the guests. "We know almost all the movements," he explains. "We can tell by how fast he takes off if he will return. If he goes straight up to the surface he is not coming back, or will stay outside. But if the mantas just circle around, they will stay as long as the divers stay down."

The position of the cephalic fins offer some clues to the mantas' intentions. For feeding they form a scoop, for rapid travel they are rolled into a spiral, and if the animals are going to stay the fins will be flared out. Fins are also used for steering. As a manta banks, one will be open, the other will be curled.

Mating season, late November through March, is a dramatic time of year in Mil Channel. The mantas form a train, with a female leading up to 20 males; whatever she does, the others follow. A few females may also join the train, but the males are chasing only the lead female. Leo states, "Sometimes when they do loops...you can see the male trying to climb on top. The male holds on only with claspers. They are together three or four minutes, the female usually trying to get away."

Jesse adds, "I have seen them mating. I have even seen sperm, it's a black cloud. The male is on top and presses the female down as they do a half or full loop." The actual mating act takes only 15 to 30 seconds. No one is certain whether a female will mate with another partner. But now that 40 individual mantas have been identified by their markings, further observations may answer the question.

During mating, males don't allow divers or anything else to come close, even displaying aggression toward each other. Leo recalled, "One of our guests kept following a big female. This male just turned around and came straight toward her. She held up the camera to take a picture, that thing just hit the camera, banging into her face. She fell on the reef and the manta stayed about 5 seconds, looking down on her before it went away. She came straight up on the boat and never even went back in the water for the camera."

Opinion is divided on the mantas' primary activity in the channels: feeding or cleaning. Leo thinks it's cleaning, although Jesse and Bill don't agree. Ragman states, "Most of the time their mouths are not open. I've never seen them eating on an outgoing tide. But on an incoming tide, you can really see the plankton in clear water.

"If they are on those certain coral heads, they are there to be cleaned. Maybe sometimes when they see plankton they open their mouths, but mostly it's a cleaning station. We have actually seen wrasses go inside the gill slits, and come out through the mouth."

Cleaning is done by wrasses and juvenile jacks. Occasionally a mimic blenny joins the cleaning station. It has markings similar to the cleaner wrasses, but uses the disguise to sneak a bite from the skin of the host. They congregate around the genitals of the manta, and the big animal quivers whenever one takes a nip.

Before the dive operation opened in 1986, Yapese men occasionally speared mantas from boats, especially in the channel between Maap and Rumung Islands. By the time they are teenagers, most Yapese can breath-hold dive to 100 feet (30 m), but these spearfishermen feared mantas because of old tales that the rays would pin people to the bottom. After some experience diving with the animals, Acker convinced the fishermen that rays presented no threat.

In three trips to Yap spread over four years, I noticed significant behavioral changes in the manta rays. They come much closer to divers now, and closer to the bottom in the middle of the channel. They are by no means tame, because they haven't been interfered with or fed; they are used to the non-intrusive presence of man. Consequently mantas seem to have learned to trust us, and a few individual rays that consistently return actually seem to seek human interaction.

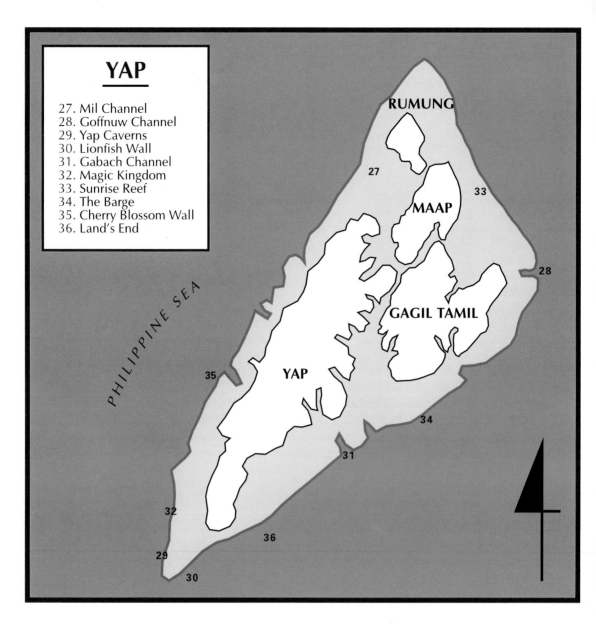

YAP

RUMUNG

MAAP

GAGIL TAMIL

YAP

PHILIPPINE SEA

DIVE SITES

27. MIL CHANNEL

DEPTH:	30-90 FEET
	(9-27 M)
LEVEL:	NOVICE TO
	ADVANCED

Mil Channel is perhaps the best known site on Yap, but is usually diveable only during the winter months. A shallow ledge at 30-foot (9 m) depth, Manta Ridge is a feeding and

cleaning station, and this is where divers wait in the current for the mantas. Find a spot and hold on tightly, because the current can really whip through here. Visibility may be up to 100 feet (30 m) on an incoming tide, an important advantage over Goofnuw where it ranges 25 to 50 feet (8-15 m). On clear days it's like being in the Grand Canyon. Stay on the bottom and near the edges of the ridge, allowing the mantas clear passage in and out of the lagoon. If you block the main cleaning area in the center, the mantas will retreat instead of making multiple passes overhead.

On a strong incoming current, a drift in from the channel mouth can be an exhilarating ride. At the entrance, depth is 140 feet (42 m) and

Tiny cleaner fishes nip parasites from the manta's skin at a cleaning station.

huge sea fans line the walls. But avoid the temptation and remain above 50 feet (15 m) to save enough air for Manta Ridge. You will drift into an area of sea whips standing vertically in the current, named the Spaghetti Factory. A point juts in to form a narrow dogleg; keep to the wall on the right to stay on course for the ridge. A resident school of pyramid butterflyfish is usually found there. Whitetip sharks may be resting along the bottom; occasional gray reef sharks, schools of parrotfish, jacks, or black snappers may be encountered as well. But look up occasionally, because you may see a manta coming, mouth open, facing into the current.

Drifting from inside on an outgoing tide is almost as exciting, but there will be a reduction in visibility. Along the north slope is a field of red gorgonians, ranging from about 30 feet (9 m) all the way to the sand channel. There is a colony of garden eels on the bottom. They are extremely shy, so just lie in the sand and watch them slowly come out of their holes, like small gray stalks waving in the current. None will come up within five feet of a diver, so forget about photographing them.

Just inside the channel from the ridge are anemone colonies with clownfishes. The side walls are decorated with hard and soft corals. There is an old piece of stone money on the bottom, dropped from a canoe years ago, lying in the sand at 70 feet (21 m). There are several fishes not seen elsewhere on Yap: schools of big barracudas, jacks and snappers, different species of blue/green parrotfish, groupers, and triggers. Whitetip sharks and eagle rays cruise the channel walls, white spotted stingrays rest on the bottom. You may see an occasional turtle. Although the usual time to dive Mil Channel is November through May, it is sometimes accessible on calm days during the summer.

28. GOOFNUW CHANNEL

DEPTH:	30-60 FEET
	(9-18 M)
LEVEL:	NOVICE TO
	ADVANCED

Goofnuw Channel, also called Valley of the Rays, is shallower than Mil, reaching only a maximum depth of 60 feet (18 m). Although visibility is not as good, there are more places to see mantas, so divers can spread out along the sand, the ridges, or behind coral heads. A sand channel runs along the bottom, and the mantas can be found anywhere along the walls or over the sand. This is usually dived on an outgoing tide, so look toward the island (northwest) for the mantas. During strong tidal changes, the mantas hover in the current over the cleaning stations, occasionally with mouths open in feeding posture. At slack current, they are likely to circle back and forth over the stations.

There are five distinct spots where the mantas go, including a large lettuce coral formation in the sand at 50 feet (15 m), a ridge on the northern wall right behind it at 25 feet (8 m), a lettuce coral formation at the base of the southern edge, and up the 30-foot (9 m) slope of that edge. There are also times they will fly right down the center of the channel. Moray eels, lobsters, nurse sharks and octopuses may also be seen among the rocks at the manta spot.

Occasionally eagle rays swim through the channel. I used to think eagle rays were graceful, but compared to mantas they seem very inefficient, flapping their wings much faster to go the same distance. The mantas are in total control of themselves, hovering effortlessly in the current while we have to hang on.

The inside limit of the manta area is a metal box, an old channel marker. When you reach that, you've gone too far. But if the mantas aren't active, follow the sand channel from there in toward the island. Beyond the manta spot in 30 to 40 feet (9-12 m) of water is a resting place for whitetip sharks. You may see upwards of 20 of these shy creatures lying in the sand, but they invariably take off when divers approach. Begging the obvious, this spot is called Shark City. Garden eels also populate the sand flats, as do nest-tending triggerfish and juvenile bristletooth surgeons in early summer.

29. YAP CAVERNS

DEPTH:	20-60 FEET
	(6-18 M)
LEVEL:	NOVICE TO
	ADVANCED

Yap Caverns is located near the island's southern tip. There are swim-throughs, surge

Dive operator Bill Acker observes schooling basslets over huge coral formations on Yap's outer reefs.

channels, and crevices, some of which have grown together into tunnels with skylights. All are wide open with plenty of daylight. The swim-throughs are nice, but it's the fishes in the sand bowls that make this dive. Around the coral pinnacles, you may encounter unicornfish, lionfish, big puffers, or jacks. Napoleon wrasses, sweetlips, groupers, goatfish, and schools of baitfish may be spotted as well. Colorful basslets (*Psuedanthias tuka*) flit around the coral like butterflies. There are occasional whitetip sharks resting in the sand, or patrolling outside when there is a strong current. The best area is about 30 feet (9 m), so don't miss it by going too deep.

30. LIONFISH WALL

DEPTH:	30-140 FEET
	(9-42 M)
LEVEL:	NOVICE TO
	ADVANCED

This sheer vertical wall dropping from 30 to 130 feet (9-39 m) and then sloping deeper, is

Although manta dives are the dominant attraction of Yap, the outside walls offer rich hard corals, fish life, and excellent visibility.

one of Yap's prime dive sites. True to its name, there are many lionfishes (*Pterois volitans*), mostly in crevices within the wall, but it's not unusual to run across one in the sand at 40 feet (12 m), near the top of the drop-off. They are docile and make beautiful photo subjects, so long as you don't corner them or reach out in a threatening gesture. Remember, they have some heavy artillery.

At the top of the drop-off is a tiny crevice which houses a group of leaf fishes. A guide is required to find it. Rare in Micronesia, this four-inch (10 cm) fish looks like a dead leaf, but is a member of the scorpionfish family and equipped with stinging spines. So don't reach out with your bare hand.

On the wall around 80 feet (24 m) is a cluster of flabby looking corallimorphian anemones. Basslets flit along the reef, and shy boxfish may be spotted in the coral. Groupers, snappers, and cruising sharks inhabit the water column beyond the wall. Mantas, turtles, eagle rays and big tuna are occasional visitors.

Twilight is a great time to make this dive. The wall is alive with action, everything looking for a final meal of the day, or trying to prevent becoming one.

Although there are things to see deep, the best diving is shallower than 50 feet (15 m).

31. GABACH CHANNEL

DEPTH:	50-150 FEET
	(15-45 M)
LEVEL:	INTERMEDIATE TO
	ADVANCED

Yap's deepest channel, Gabach (ga BOSH) is supposed to be the site of a Japanese bomber wreck, but it has yet to be found. There are empty artillery shells on the sand bottom at 150 feet (45 m), which may have started the rumor. But you don't have to go deep to make this a good dive. Outside the channel, a mini-wall plateaus at about 65 feet (20 m) in sand, then drops again to 150 (45 m). Along the wall are hard coral formations, mounds, swim-throughs and overhangs, all decorated with large sea fans, leather corals and sea whips. A school of hammerheads has been reported here. Nurse sharks commonly hide in crevices on the bottom and along the wall, and gray reef sharks cruise outside.

Mantas have been seen here in late afternoon when the tide is coming in, but their appearance isn't predictable like Mil and Goofnuw. Because of its proximity to the harbor, this is a popular site for night diving.

32. MAGIC KINGDOM

DEPTH:	30-60 FEET
	(9-18 M)
LEVEL:	NOVICE TO
	ADVANCED

The delicate lettuce and staghorn corals which once decorated the shallow area of Magic Kingdom's sloping wall were severely damaged by a typhoon in November 1992. There is evidence of new growth, but it may take years for this site to return to its former glory.

A mini-wall begins from the surface to about 15 to 20 feet (5-6 m), then gently slopes to 60 (18 m). At 45 feet (14 m) is a big crevice in the reef flat, and in the middle is an undercut coral pinnacle. A series of gullies houses several different types of anemones, clownfishes in every one. Among the interesting fishes found there are slingjaw and birdnose wrasses, clown triggers, and naso surgeons. A school of giant bumphead parrotfish munch on the corals and defecate clouds of sand.

In a strong current, there can be excellent water column action here. Schools of jacks may be mating in summer. Males turn black while courting, so look for a black and a silver fish swimming together. Separate schools of big and small barracudas, solitary tunas, snappers, and rainbow runners all compete for space. Sharks, turtles and Napoleon wrasses are among the residents.

Caution. In strong currents this site is for advanced divers only.

33. SUNRISE REEF

DEPTH:	30-70 FEET
	(9-21 M)
LEVEL:	NOVICE TO
	ADVANCED

Yap has outstanding hard coral formations, and some of the most beautiful are found at Sunrise Reef, north of the entrance to Goofnuw Channel. Layers of yellow and green lettuce coral, and blue antler corals add touches of color to the landscape. Dome and table corals are also present. Parallel sand channels run through the coral ridges, forming small canyons at depths of 50 to 70 feet (15-21 m), with the tops of the ridges at 30 to 50 feet (9-15 m). Colorful reef fishes dart among the corals.

This is an excellent area for reef fish photography. There are big schools of pyramid butterflies, many anemones housing clownfish, slingjaw wrasses, and sweetlips. Huge schools of bumphead parrotfishes commonly swim through. In the water column, look for schools of jacks, bigeye emperors and batfish.

The best time to dive this spot is late afternoon, when the fishes are very active. It is often done after a manta dive at Goofnuw Channel. Other names sometimes used for this site are Bill's Reef and Cabbage Patch. This part of the island is buffeted by wind seven months of the year, so it is strictly a summertime dive.

34. THE BARGE

DEPTH:	50-75 FEET
	(15-21 M)
LEVEL:	NOVICE TO
	ADVANCED

Located just outside the harbor entrance, this is a convenient spot for night dives, or as a second site after a manta dive. It gets its name from a sunken barge that sits on top of the reef. There is a gradually sloping wall of hard coral formations, mostly domes and plates, leveling out about 90 feet (27 m). The best features are big coral mounds. It's a good spot to shoot pictures of flame gobies, clownfish in anemones and rainbow wrasses.

At night, there are crinoids, sleeping parrotfishes, dogface puffers, groupers and rabbitfishes. Moorish idols and butterflyfishes are in their night colors. The butterflies seem in sort of a twilight zone, not asleep but not really awake.

35. CHERRY BLOSSOM WALL

DEPTH:	20-150 FEET (6-45 M)
LEVEL:	NOVICE TO ADVANCED

A sheer drop-off, beginning at 20 feet (6 m) and going to about 160 (50 m), this site gets its name from the profusion of tunicates in shallow water. It is usually done as a drift, with the best diving about the 60-foot (18 m) level. Look into crevices for shy critters. Snappers, jacks, sharks and unicornfish swim in open water. Sea fans, up to four feet across, attest to the strength of the currents. In deeper water below 120 feet (36 m), there are large black coral trees and even larger sea fans.

The shallow area is good for reef fish photography, with lots of anemones and clownfish, parrots including bumpheads, and flame gobies. Even during the daytime, there are lots of open crinoids. But don't forget to check outside water for sharks and schooling fishes.

36. LAND'S END

DEPTH:	20-90 FEET (6-27 M)
LEVEL:	NOVICE TO ADVANCED

Above 60 feet (18 m) the wall slopes gently with lots of coral outcrops and big coral domes, then gives way to a vertical drop-off. In the shallows, the slope is cut by sand canyons, where you may run into the elusive crocodile fishes. There is one big area of dead coral. Bumphead parrotfish and flame gobies are among interesting reef fishes. Schools of barracudas, sharks, snappers and unicorn surgeonfish swim in open water.

Just south of this site is Eagle's Nest, a coral head in 50 feet (15 m) that is regularly patrolled by two or three spotted eagle rays. A sandy bottom slopes to about 130 feet (39 m), but optimum depth for this dive is 50 to 60 feet (15-18 m). It is usually done as the second dive of the day, so most people stay shallow. Guides often begin a drift at Land's End and wind up at Eagle's Nest.

The unicorn surgeonfish, Naso annulatus, is usually found swimming next to steep drop-offs, at depths of 75 feet (23 m) and more. The horn can be used as an offensive and defensive weapon.

CHAPTER **VI** PALAU

AT A GLANCE

Even before there was diving, Palau had captured the imagination of writers, photographers, artists, and the few fortunate travelers who got there. It's truly a land of superlatives. Today this island nation appears on virtually everybody's list of the world's best diving places, usually right near the top.

It seems incredible that so much natural beauty can be concentrated in one place. There are the magical Rock Islands and white sand beaches where you can find solitude, as well as good restaurants and hotels where you can find people. Underwater, the descriptive word is diversity. There are the wall and current dives that everybody associates with Palau, with so many sharks that after a while you virtually take them for granted. But there's more: over 50 Japanese shipwrecks from World War II, an underwater cave, an arch filled with soft corals, a marine lake filled with jellyfish, thrilling current rides through sand channels, and a vertical tunnel.

The 20-mile (32 km) long lagoon between Koror (ko ROAR) and Peleliu is dotted by over 200 tiny rock islands, the keystone feature of Palau. Covered with luxuriant jungle growth, they look like green mushrooms on the crystalline blue of the lagoon. Most are dome-shaped, many undercut by thousands of years of rasping by chitons and grazing fishes. Toward the southern end of the lagoon some are fringed by white sand beaches. The daily ride to the dive site through the Rock Islands is one of the highlights of the Palau experience.

The wonders of Palau were first brought to the attention the diving public in the lyrical, mystical photographs of Douglas Faulkner in the 1960's and 70's. At that time accommodations were primitive and diving required a full-scale expedition. Today, Koror is one of Micronesia's big cities, and there is a well-developed infrastructure for tourism.

The Republic of Palau (Belau, in local language) was the last of the former trust territories to gain its independence, finally ratifying the Compact of Free Association with the United States in 1994. Under its provisions, U.S. subsidies are being phased out over 15 years, so Palau has turned to Japan for new sources of income. Luxury hotels are being built on Babeldaob (BAB el dop), the largest island, which was mostly jungle. A new perimeter road now under construction will enhance development.

On the surface, Palau's capitol, Koror, is very westernized. People dress like we do, and there are more late-model cars, pickup trucks, and powerboats than on any Micronesian island with comparable population. But Palauan people are hard to get to know. Beneath the veneer of representative government is a complex society that the visitor doesn't see. The ancient clan system still prevails. There are numerous obligations to the extended family, and a money system that goes back hundreds of years, worn today by women in the form of bead jewelry. According to Francis Toribiong, founder of Palau's oldest dive operation (Fish 'n Fins) and a tribal chief, "If you want to know the family history, ask to see their money."

Palauans are reserved around foreigners, and saving face is of paramount importance. Divers may be frustrated by terse briefings of guides,

Colorful soft corals, Dendroephythya sp., are the crowning glory of Indo-Pacific reefs. Calcium spicules help support the structures in strong currents, upon which they depend for nutrients.

STORYBOARDS

The most popular souvenir of Palau is a storyboard, an intricate relief wood carving, depicting one of the islands' many folk legends. They originated during the Japanese occupation when an anthropologist, Hisakatsu Hijikata, taught people to carve copies of the paintings that decorated their *bais* (men's houses). The best ones today are made by inmates of the Koror jail, where master carvers train other prisoners in return for a share of their sale prices. Prices are negotiable, sometimes with the carver himself. Good ones aren't cheap; expect to pay over $100 for quality work. Quality and prices vary tremendously, so shop around before you buy. The storyboard illustrated here was carved by Lucius L. Malsol, a prison inmate, and illustrates the legend of the magical breadfruit tree.

THE FISH-BEARING TREE OF NGIBTAL

In the ancient days there was an island named Ngibtal (Many Palauan names begin with the letters "Ng." The g is silent.) near the village of Ngiwal. On its shore an old woman lived alone. She had a son, but he was hardly ever home because he constantly had to travel to the other villages. The people of Ngibtal used to pass by the home of the old woman each day as they returned from the sea with their catch, but no one ever offered her any of their fish. One day after a particularly long absence, her son came home to visit, and the old  woman complained that while others had plenty to eat, she never had a fish for her pot. Before setting out on his next trip, he went out into the yard of his mother's house, and chopped off one of the branches of a breadfruit tree growing next to the water's edge. Water immediately began to gush from the trunk, flowing with the rhythm of the waves on the shore. With each surge, a fish leaped out. The miraculous tree became the envy of all the other people on the island. They complained, "While we must go out to sea for our fish, the old woman can get all she wishes by sitting under her tree." Finally one night, an old man stole over to the wonderful fish-bearing tree and chopped it down. The water that used to flow intermittently now burst out in a torrent and soon the entire island was flooded. To this day, the site of the island with its stone pathways and platforms can be seen from the water's surface off the shore of Ngiwal on Babeldaob Island.

Francis Toribiong discovered many of the sites we enjoy today.

At Oolong Beach, trees seem to grow out of bare rock.

often limited to, "Keep the wall on your left." According to Francis, "We don't want to explain everything, and sometimes it turns out to be completely wrong...We don't know what's really happening every moment, so we give just enough information (to be) safe. Also, we want to surprise people; we want them to have the feeling of being first. I do not claim (to have) discovered a lot of things, because my forefathers were here before. I was just fortunate enough to have a diving mask. They were fishing at Peleliu (PEL e loo) Wall, they knew wrecks sank somewhere out there, but never had time to find them. So I never feel I have the honor of finding this place, I just follow my father's steps."

WEATHER

Weather patterns are dominated by northeast tradewinds from December through June. Blue Corner and Ngemilis are in the lee during that time. The rest of the year, winds may come from any direction. Typhoons usually pass to northeast, but can occur any time. During the rainy season there are usually three days of excellent diving, a day or two of building seas, a couple days of rough weather, a couple days of settling, then the pattern repeats.

A windbreaker worn over the wetsuit cuts down evaporative cooling and is important for comfort on rainy days. When it's blowing hard, operators based in Koror usually dive the east coast or the harbor shipwrecks. East coast sites include Coral Garden, Ngerong, Short Drop-off, Lighthouse Channel and Whiteface.

THINGS TO DO ON LAND

The **Belau National Museum** in Koror, though small, does an excellent job of interpreting the nation's history and culture. It's a good place to visit early in your trip to gain some insight to Palau's traditions. Among the most interesting exhibits are paintings of Palauan life by local artist Charlie Gibbons, rendered in a primitive,

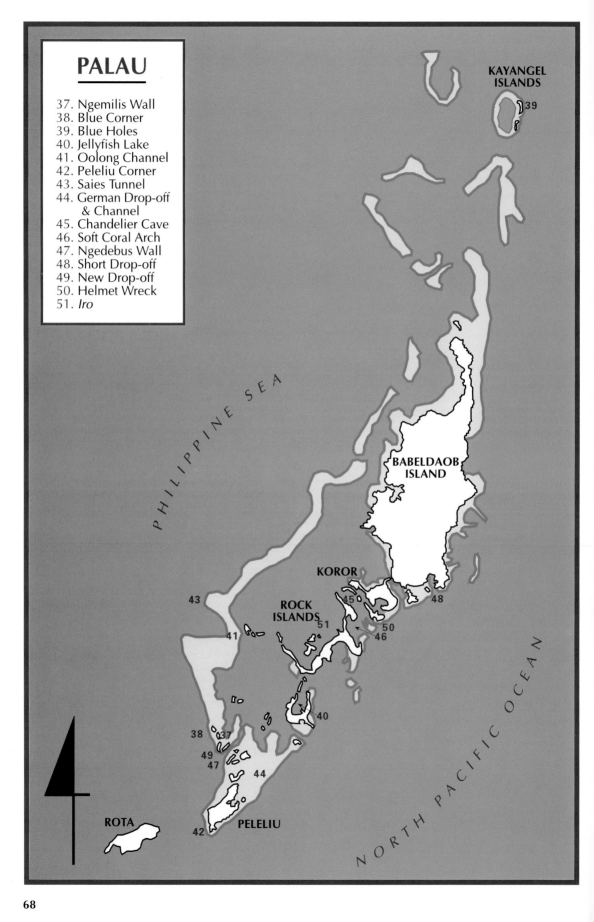

PALAU

KAYANGEL
ISLANDS

39

PHILIPPINE SEA

BABELDAOB
ISLAND

KOROR

43

ROCK
ISLANDS

51

41

45

48

50
46

40

38 37

49
47

44

ROTA

42 PELELIU

NORTH PACIFIC OCEAN

Grandma Moses style. On the grounds is a reconstructed bai (by), or traditional meeting house. Most bais on Palau today are contemporary structures, so this the best opportunity to see one the way they used to be.

You can rent a car for a day and explore **Babeldaob**, the largest island in Micronesia besides Guam. The island is divided into ten states, most of which built networks of roads, that aren't necessarily connected to those of the next state, until the completion of the new road. On top of a hill overlooking the island are four large **Japanese cannons** with a commanding view of the pass into the lagoon. One is in a pillbox with concrete about 2 feet (.6 m) thick; all are heavily shielded in semi-circular armor. Another dirt road leads to a bombed-out **Japanese headquarters**, with three anti-aircraft guns and a rusting tank outside. Nearby is a modern bai, beautifully decorated with paintings of Palauan legends. Both these sites are located near the airport.

The **Micronesian Mariculture Demonstration Center** on Koror, where they raise *Tridacna* (giant clams), was the first of its kind in Micronesia. Now self sustaining, there is no longer need to take any clams from the wild; all are hatched from brood stock. Living off symbiotic algae and what they filter from seawater, they take care of themselves; all they need is fresh seawater pumped through the tanks. The clams are raised in tanks for two years, then transplanted into a protected area of the lagoon. The leading market is the aquarium trade, next is Japanese sushi bars, third is seed stock to other labs. The lab is open to visitors on weekdays.

Sightseeing flights over the **Rock Islands** can be arranged on a charter basis. The aircraft door is removed for unhindered photography. It's expensive, but sharing the cost makes it more feasible. A more economical way to see the islands from the air is to buy a round trip ticket from Koror to Peleliu on Air Paradise.

There is a self-guided **nature trail** at the **Palau Pacific Resort**, that takes about 45 minutes to cover on foot. It winds through a lily pond, a dam built by the Japanese, up log stair-steps, and through thick jungle foliage. Not too strenuous, it's an easy introduction to Palau's rain forest. The Palau Pacific is worth a visit, even if you aren't staying there. It has fine restaurants, shops, and recreational facilities.

Another way to encounter the rain forest is a **day trip to a rock island**. Your group will be dropped off on an island in the morning with a picnic lunch, then left on your own and picked up when the dive boats head home. You can explore, snorkel, swim, or just loaf on the beach. All your fantasies of a Pacific island hideaway will be realized.

Koror has a variety of **restaurants**, most with oriental themes. A common feature, and one of the cheapest items on the menu, is sashimi. This Japanese raw fish dish is usually yellowfin tuna that had been swimming that afternoon. Eaten with soy sauce and wasabe, it melts in your mouth, with absolutely no fishy taste. Even the presentation is elegant, with chunks of fish on one side of the tray, and thin slivers arranged like flowers on the other.

Koror has a 12:30 A.M. curfew for cars, enforced by the local police. The purpose is to discourage drunkenness, but isn't always successful as Palauans drive aggressively when they've had too much. This shouldn't be a problem for dedicated divers, who need to get up in time to make the 9 A.M. boat.

DIVING

Land-based, a typical day's diving routine begins at 9 A.M. for the hour's boat ride to one of the walls outside the lagoon. The speedy vessels go about 25 knots in the protected waters, often weaving in and out of the shallow water between the spectacular Rock Islands. In contrast to a rough, featureless open water trip, these boat rides are an enjoyable part of the Palau diving experience.

After the morning dive, you are brought to a sandy beach on an island inside the lagoon for a leisurely picnic lunch. The afternoon dive is usually inside the lagoon, but if customers request and conditions permit, another wall dive can be made instead. The "short" dives: Jellyfish Lake, Chandelier Cave, or Soft Coral Arch may be done on the way home if prior arrangements have been made. Instead of bringing a third tank, divers are asked to save 500 to 1000 psi (35-69 bar) for these dives.

Land-based operations offer only two dives a day, while up to five may be made from a live-aboard boats. Live-aboards offer the advantage of diving more remote sites like northern Babeldaob, Angaur, and Kayangel Islands, in addition to night dives, which are difficult to arrange when land-based.

Diver Mia Tegner hovers behind a huge sea fan on Ngemelis Wall.

A number of land-based operations compete for divers' business on Palau. The longest established is **Fish 'n Fins**, based at the Marina Hotel. Founder Francis Toribiong discovered many of Palau's dive sites and wrecks. Shallum and Mandy Eptisons's **Neco Marine** is at a marina on Malakal Island. Mandy has written a series of books on Palau's cultural, natural, and underwater heritage. **Splash** is a modern facility located on the palatial grounds of the Palau Pacific Resort. **Sam's Tours**, owned by Sam Scott, offers personalized service for smaller groups. In addition to a full service dive shop, they offer kayaking and land tours. Initially geared toward Japanese guests, **Carp Island Resort** now serves an international clientelle in rustic cottages on their own island. It's located near the prime dive sites of Blue Corner and Ngemelis Wall, so they can dive it early in the morning before other operations get there.

In addition there are several live-aboards: *Palau Aggressor II, Sun Dancer II, Ocean Hunter, Palau Sport* and *Big Blue Explorer.*

Wreck Diving

People intending to dive World War II shipwrecks generally go to Truk, but Palau has its share as well. Many are located in the harbor, a 20-minute boat ride from Koror. These wrecks are usually visited on rainy days, when divers and guides prefer shorter boat trips. Because of conditions in the harbor, these ships lack the lush, beautiful soft coral growth of Truk's wrecks. The mood is dark and somber, with visibility in the 30- to 50-foot (9-15 m) range. Yet the wrecks are covered with profuse marine growth including sawtooth clams, corals, and *Tridacna* on the shallow superstructure. The fauna of the quiet harbor waters is very different from that of the outer reefs. The predominant living shape is a branching gorgonian, a form of black coral, with colors dominated by earth tones of browns and muddy yellows. Schools of barracudas, batfish, fusiliers and damsels swim about the hulls.

DIVE SITES

37. NGEMILIS WALL

DEPTH:	10-140 FEET
	(3-12 M)
LEVEL:	NOVICE TO
	ADVANCED

One of the world's most famous wall dives, this is called "Big Drop-off" by the locals. A vertical wall over 800 feet (242 m) deep, Ngemilis (NEM i lis) is the southern extension of a barrier reef structure running from Blue Hole to German Channel. Enormous sea fans, fed by the current, are spread out at varying depths, seemingly a bigger one always a few feet further down. The largest in Palau, located here at 95 feet (29 m), is nearly 20 feet (6 m) across.

Most of the wall is alive with rich invertebrate growth, soft corals providing most of the color. Black coral trees and plate corals are very much in evidence. Reef fishes lead a vertical existence, especially in the shallow water. There are lots of sweetlips, yellow trumpetfish, blue-square fairy basslets, and the usual butterflies and angels. A lot of cleaning activity goes on here.

Be careful of your depth and bottom time, because it is tempting to go too deep. The best part of this dive is above 60 feet (18 m). When the current is strong, open water activity increases, especially where sharks are concerned. It's a long wall, but as you continue to drift, you can stop at scenic spots

to enjoy the gorgonians and fishes. The shallow reef fish population is extremely rich, making the safety stop an enjoyable part of the dive. A variety of groupers, angelfishes, black surgeons, big boxfish, and blue-square fairy basslets are concentrated at depths above 25 feet (8 m).

38. BLUE CORNER

DEPTH:	30-130 FEET
	(9-39 M)
LEVEL:	ADVANCED

The most renowned dive site in Palau, Blue Corner is renowned for sheer electricity and excitement. This is the place for high-energy open water action, especially when the current is running. The wall itself is beautiful, but there is so much going on outside that divers hardly notice. Countless sharks cruise the blue water, mostly whitetips, blacktips, and gray reef sharks, but also lots of full-bodied silvertips. In deep water, living whirlpools of large jacks school for protection from predators. Eagle rays, tunas, and schools of barracudas are frequent visitors. The sharks seem fat and happy with the bonanza of fishes surrounding the wall. They ignore divers, preferring to maintain about 30 feet (9 m) of personal space while hunting their next meal. When a couple of sharks turn on the horsepower and dash after something, schools of planktivores suddenly dash for the protection of the wall.

At 50 feet (15m) is an observation platform, a flat spot on top of the wall where divers can hang on and watch the show below. The stronger the currrent, the better the action, so sometimes getting to the edge of the platform requires pulling yourself along the bottom, hand over hand. Don't worry about damaging the coral, because the gloves and knees of thousands of divers have already wiped it out. Once you reach the edge of the wall, use your reef hook.

Invented by a dive guide at Sam's Tours, reef hooks are now used by all dive operators. It's a big fish hook with the barb and point ground off, on a four- to five-foot (1.2-1.5 m) line. A brass clip at the other end is attached to your BC. Divers set the hook into a dead part of the

At Blue Corner, divers hang on to the edge of the wall to watch sharks and other pelagics. The stronger the current, the better the show.

reef, then hang in the current with both hands free. This protects the reef and the divers' hands, allowing stability while watching the show.

If you are approaching the corner from the north in a strong current, it is best to stay at 70 feet (21 m) or so, well below the observation platform. Blue Corner is on a point facing the full force of the wind and the swell. Tons of water are forced up the steep wall, and over that ledge. The current becomes intense there, and an unwary diver who is too shallow will be swept up and over the platform before he knows what's happening.

Like many drift dives in Palau, this ends with a live boat pickup, sometimes in heavy swells. That's when you appreciate the skill and efficiency of the Palauan skippers. To make their job easier, swim away from the reef and toward open water for pickup.

39. BLUE HOLES

DEPTH:	20-110 FEET
	(6-33 M)
LEVEL:	INTERMEDIATE TO
	ADVANCED

A spectacular vertical cavern with three overhead skylights and two deep exits, Blue Holes is located just north of Blue Corner. Typically the dive plan begins with a dive in Blue Holes and utilizes the drift along the outer

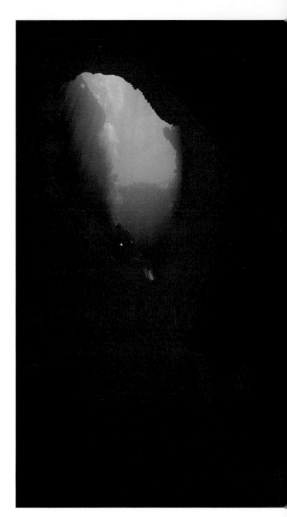

Blue Holes is a dramatic vertical cavern with three skylights.

wall for safety decompression. This works best if the current is slack, allowing divers to enjoy the reef fish and invertebrates along the wall.

Entry is through any one of three skylights on top of the reef, ranging from 15 to 30 feet (5-9 m) deep. They lead into a vast vertical cavern, dropping some 80 feet (24 m) to a sand bottom at 110 feet (33m). Shafts of sunlight filtering through the openings evoke the aura of a submerged cathedral.

Photo tip. If you need an image to bring back home, use the widest angle lens you have, fast film, and a shutter speed of at least 1/125 to freeze the sun rays. Shut down the strobe and let ambient light take over.

There are two exits to the outside, one at 80 feet (24 m), the other at the bottom. Keeping the wall on your left, begin ascending and enjoy its vertical world. Vast aggregations of pyramid butterflies and red-tooth triggers hover along the wall. Plankton feeding fusiliers, snappers, triggers, and damsels are abundant. Anemones with clownfish are found on ledges, and the occasional Napoleon wrasse swims through. Snapper and barracuda schools swim through outside water, along with the ever-present sharks. If you have spent any amount of time in the cavern, you will run out of air before reaching Blue Corner. That's just as well, because it's worth a dive all its own.

40. JELLYFISH LAKE

DEPTH:	0-10 FEET
	(0-3 M)
LEVEL:	NOVICE TO
	ADVANCED

The 1998 El Nino raised temperatures in Jellyfish Lake into the mid-90's (34-36°C), and killed the animals that made this marine lake famous. According to Sam Scott, there had been similar die-offs during prior El Ninos, and the jellyfish came back. But this was the most severe incidence, and recovery is uncertain. Snorkelers are still brought into the lake for its unusual, ethereal beauty. The following description was written before the die-off.

Jellyfish Lake is a trip back through time, to a primordial era when the earth was young. A marine lake in the center of a Rock Island, this is home to an isolated population of small jellyfish. With no predators over millennia, these animals have lost their ability to sting. Consequently, divers can swim among thousands of them with no problems.

It is best to make this dive on sunny days because the jellyfish concentrate in the center of the lake. But rain can lend an aura of mystery and primeval timelessness to the experience, even though the jellyfish are more spread out.

The journey begins with a short swim to Eil Malik Island from your dive boat anchored offshore. Then you climb the rocky, muddy

Jellyfish Lake is filled with thousands of fist-sized Mastiguis *jellyfish. With no predators they no longer can sting, although their relatives in unprotected waters retain the ability.*

Gray reef sharks are common throughout Micronesia. A juvenile glides through a sunburst in Palau's shallows.

slope of the hill surrounding the lake. Wear a strong pair of booties. About 100 feet (30 m) high, the path snakes through jungle, with mud, sharp limestone rocks, and roots forming formidable obstacles. This is a skin dive, and hikers will be thankful not to be burdened with tanks and weight belts. Entry is though a narrow mangrove channel, obstructed by sunken logs that can't be seen in the dark water with less than 3-foot (1 m) visibility. Tales of salt-water crocodiles that lurk there won't enhance your peace of mind, but they hunt at night and are rarely seen by visitors.

Visibility improves as you kick toward the center of the lake. Rain and runoff produce a freshwater lens, about 4 to 6 inches (10-15 cm) deep, lying on top of denser but warmer salt water. The resulting halocline distorts vision, but soon you begin to see an occasional jellyfish. When viewed from the side they are apricot-colored; from below they are translucent and constantly pulsating, the small ones faster than the larger ones. Near the center of the lake, the numbers gradually increase until there are thousands of them, like being in the middle of an arcade game surrounded by tiny orange spaceships. They feel smooth and silky to the touch, making no apparent effort to avoid divers. Surface dives reveal them to be concentrated within the first 6 feet (2 m) of the water column, with an occasional bowl-shaped, transparent *Aurelia* among them. There are also a few cardinalfish, but they prey only on tiny, injured jellyfish.

These jellyfish belong to the genus *Mastigius*; whose relatives are found throughout Palau Lagoon and possess a powerful sting. This population, trapped eons ago, evolved into what we see today: an animal with tiny, clublike tentacles whose remaining sting (if any) is too weak to be felt by man. A symbiotic alga grows in its tissues. On bright days, the colony follows the sun around the lake, individuals slowly rotating counterclockwise to allow all the algae within their bodies to photosynthesize.

41. OOLONG CHANNEL

DEPTH:	50-70 FEET
	(15-21 M)
LEVEL:	INTERMEDIATE TO
	ADVANCED

Sometimes overlooked among Palau's great variety of diving experiences, Oolong Channel is an unsung gem. It begins rather ordinarily, on a dull-colored wall, that turns out to be a hunting ground for sharks. Then you enter a sand channel that cuts through the fringing reef and are swept along on a wild current ride, past fantastic coral formations covered by colorful invertebrates and home to hordes of reef fishes.

This dive should be done on an incoming tide, which greatly improves visibility and creates the adrenaline rush of the current drift. When the tide is going out, visibility is poor and it is virtually impossible to enter the channel against the current. The boats usually drop divers on the wall outside the channel, with only the admonition, "Keep the wall on your left." Avoid the temptation to go too deep. It's best to cruise at 60 feet (18 m) or so and save your air for the channel drift. But keep your eyes open for sharks. This is an excellent spot to observe shark behavior, including gray reef sharks hunting and whitetips mating. In contrast to the casual cruising of sharks at other times, feeding movements tend to be aggressive and purposeful, although divers have nothing to fear as long as they stay along the wall.

The sandy bottom gradually rises to 60 feet (18 m) where it forms the entrance to the channel. Here the current takes over and propels divers through the channel. Islands of hard coral formations are scattered in the sand, decorated with colorful soft corals. To get a closer look, try facing backward occasionally and kicking to hold your position. That will work except in narrow passages or at the height of the flow.

Late spring and early summer is mating time for groupers, when they are seemingly everywhere in the channel, ranging in size from two footers (62 cm) to 100-pound (45 kg) behemoths. As you fly through, they are spooked out of the open and dart into crevices and holes.

Because of the vigorous water movement, the general shape and depths of the sandy bottom, coral growth, and predominant animals are constantly shifting. Maximum intensity is at around 30 feet (9 m), where the channel narrows. As it widens toward the lagoon side, the current diminishes and you are spilled into a broad sandy plain, home to a colony of garden eels and occasional resting whitetip sharks.

42. PELELIU CORNER

DEPTH:	30-100 FEET
	(9-30 M)
LEVEL:	ADVANCED

Caution. This high-energy drift dive is extremely weather dependent, and a challenge for even the most experienced divers. Because the southern tip of Peleliu offers no weather protection, it can be done only in calm seas. Even then, pickup is difficult and totally dependent on the skill of the boat operators. A signal float for each diver is recommended.

The currents feed an incredibly rich growth of giant sea fans and black coral along the wall. The best black coral trees are below 100 feet (30 m). A large portion of the wall is covered by tiny yellow anemones. Whip corals, jutting out from the wall like coiled springs, are covered with huge crinoids in outrageous yellows, blues, and pastels.

Avoid the temptation to go too deep; save your air for the corner. About 60 to 70 feet (18-21 m) is optimum depth. As you near the corner, the current picks up, and so do the sharks. Be careful not to go too shallow here, because before you realize it, the current can pick you up and toss you over the reeftop. Try to find a spot to hang on at around 60 feet (18 m), then stop and watch the show.

In the outer water are Napoleon wrasses, big groupers, schooling jacks, snappers, triggers, and sharks: whitetip, silvertip, blacktip, and gray reef sharks. When the current is slack, this can become a pleasant drift along a colorful wall, with fairy basslets and other reef fish providing lots of closeup photo opportunities.

Peleliu Corner was the site of Palau's most tragic diving accident, when five divers were swept away by the current and drifted to their death in the open ocean. They had chartered a local fishing boat, because no licensed dive operator would take them there that day. This dive requires sound judgement and skill on the part of divers, guides, and boat crew.

43. SAIES TUNNEL

DEPTH:	30-140 FEET
	(9-42 M)
LEVEL:	ADVANCED

Saies (SI ez) tunnel is a vertical cavern with three deep entrances and a deeper exit. The largest and most spectacular entrance is an arch at 90 feet (27 m), the shallowest is about 80 feet (24 m). Black coral trees surround this hole and cover the ceiling. Sea fans and crinoids decorate the inner walls and the overhang outside the exit. There is plenty of ambient light inside the cavern, but a flashlight will accentuate the colors. The sand bottom at 137 feet (42 m) is a forest of towering sea fans, black coral trees, and some of the biggest sea whips you will ever see. Schools of jacks hang around the tunnel exit, and whitetip sharks often rest in the sand on the bottom. From there, the dive plan is to swim back up along the wall for safety decompression because of the time spent at depth. Like many of Palau's walls, it has a rich covering of invertebrates and is home to myriad reef fishes, making the safety stop a pleasant part of the dive.

44. GERMAN DROP-OFF & CHANNEL

DEPTH:	10-110 FEET
	(3-33 M)
LEVEL:	NOVICE TO
	ADVANCED

The best part of this dive is the sloping wall leading into the channel, which is excellent for watching and photographing reef fishes and coral formations. Dominated by antler corals, it begins at 10 feet (3 m) and gradually drops to about 120 feet (36 m) before leveling off into sand. Following the wall, you can eventually drift into the channel, but the best area for viewing reef fishes and coral formations is between 50 and 30 feet (15 and 9 m).

In deeper water there are big groupers, pretty purple and white mushroom corals, bicolor angels, many butterflies, and blackfin dartfishes. The slope rises into a broad plain at about 30 feet (9 m), covered with beautiful hard coral formations. These include some table corals and more rounded ones in yellows, tans, and light blues, resembling something out of Tolkein. Clown triggers, filefish, and boxfish

---

PELELIU ISLAND

The site of one of the bloodiest battles of World War II, Peleliu Island is sometimes used for a long lunch stop, allowing time to explore. In the Camp Beck Dock are rusting hulks of landing craft, including one that is supposed to have been used by General Douglas MacArthur. Bullet casings can still be found by wading in the shallow water. There is a maze of crushed coral roads and airstrips. By prior arrangement, truck rides can be arranged to Bloody Nose Ridge, where the remains of bunkers, artillery, and tanks can still be seen. Twelve thousand troops died in this battle.

are some of the resident fishes. Schools of bignose unicornfish cruise above the corals. A few giant *Tridacna* clams, with beautiful patterns of symbiotic algae in their mantles, can be found here. Many colorful crinoids, with yellow, black, and light green patterns, perch on top of the coral, and are open even during the day.

The channel itself, blasted by the Germans in the early 20th century, is sometimes done as a drift dive. Mantas may be encountered here, but they are far more wary than those of Yap. The outer slope at 50 feet (15 m) and shallower, with fantastic hard coral gardens, is the highlight of this dive.

45. CHANDELIER CAVE

DEPTH:	10-35 FEET
	(3-11 M)
LEVEL:	INTERMEDIATE TO
	ADVANCED

This is usually done on the way home, so save about 1000 psi (69 bar). The entry is the deepest point; most of the dive is from 10 to 20 feet (3-6 m). This is a true cave; you are dependent upon the guide to find the way back out because you can't always see daylight from inside. There are four chambers connected by narrow passageways, and divers are usually taken only into the outer two. It's a classic cave, with stalactites and stalagmites in crystalline visibility. On entering, the water feels cold, but is actually 78 degrees (26°C). It tastes salty, but is actually a freshwater lens sitting on top of the denser salt water. About 10 feet (3 m) down is a halocline, where everything fuzzes out, like looking through Jell-O. Then suddenly you are in warm, 85 degree (29°C) relatively clear saltwater. There are several air pockets, and with fresh air filtering through the porous limestone, it is safe to stick your head up there and breathe. These pockets are caves in the making, with stalactites, dripstones, and soda-straws in varying shades of color and striations.

This is as far as most divers ever get to go. With special arrangement, it is possible to have a guide take you into the fourth chamber, where you can climb out of the water and

At a depth of only 20 feet (6 m), Chandelier Cave can be dived on the last few hundred pounds of air after a day of diving Palau's reefs.

explore the dry cave under the island. Obviously, this requires a full tank, backup lights, and a guide who knows the cave.

46. SOFT CORAL ARCH

DEPTH:	15-30 FEET
	(5-9 M)
LEVEL:	NOVICE TO
	ADVANCED

This dive is done as a brief excursion on the way home, and divers are asked to save 500 psi (35 bar) from the last regular dive. It could also be done as a free dive. The arch is above the surface, the passage below is lined with the biggest, healthiest soft corals you will find in Palau, mostly in shades of pastels. A slight current brings nourishment, and maintains visibility in the 30- to 50-foot (9-15 m) range, despite its location close to Koror. Ambient light is nearly nil, and divers' exhalations dislodge a rain of material from the ceiling, making photography difficult. You can enjoy the entire site in five to ten minutes.

47. NGEDEBUS WALL

DEPTH:	15-100 FEET (5-30 M)
LEVEL:	NOVICE TO ADVANCED

Located across the channel from Ngemelis, Ngedebus (NED e boos) is a gentle wall, with interesting hard coral formations and an extraordinary amount of reef fish action. It is similar to Ngemelis, with not quite the rich soft corals and sea fans. There is less current here, and fewer pelagics, although the occasional gray reef shark will cruise by.

Among the reef fishes are sixbar angelfish, yellow trumpetfish, clown triggers, and bicolor angels. Slingjaw wrasses, who can extrude their jaw several inches, are also common. Planktivores in the water colum include fusiliers, huge aggregations of pyramid butterflies, and fairy basslets.

Large cuttlefish, two to three feet long, sometimes hang around. They typically hover along the reef, all the while flashing subtle color changes. When a cuttlefish wants to move a bit faster it opens its circular siphon, located just below the tentacles, looking like a Betty Boop mouth.

Other common invertebrates are anemones with clownfish, soft corals, crinoids, and plate corals. Blackfin dartfish hover above the reef, their tiny mouths gulping plankton. Juvenile dartfish appear in aggregations; adults in pairs.

The wall is a series of steps, with table corals on the flat areas and sea fans on the deep vertical ones. Just north of Ngedebus is Turtle Cove, and occasional sea turtles cruise this area as well.

The outer corner of the reef is where the drop-off is the steepest, and that's the best place to begin the dive.

48. SHORT DROP-OFF

DEPTH:	30-130+ FEET (9-39+ M)
LEVEL:	NOVICE TO ADVANCED

This site gets its name because it's a short boat trip from the docks. Located on the eastern side of the islands, it is usually dived when winds prevent diving the Ngemelis side. Healthy sea fans and soft corals indicate that currents here are not unusual. The wall has a gradual slope until about 60 feet (18 m), where it becomes steeper. Some of the best diving is in the shallow coral gardens, with colorful invertebrates and reef fish. This is often done as the first dive on Palau. Only advanced divers should dive this site in strong current.

49. NEW DROP-OFF

DEPTH:	35-130 FEET (11-39 M)
LEVEL:	NOVICE TO ADVANCED

This is also called West Ngemilis. The wall begins at 35 to 40 feet (11-12 m), a reef table of damaged coral, with hordes of grazing parrotfish including big bumpheads. The best reef fish activity is from there to about 50 feet (15 m), where moorish idols, fusiliers, coronetfish, groupers, sweetlips, and butterflyfish abound. Schools of blueline snappers swirl around divers. In the waters above the reef are hordes of pyramid butterflies, many being cleaned. Moving out from the wall are unicorn surgeonfishes, jacks, and barracudas. In outer waters, schools of snappers share space with cruising gray reef sharks.

The best invertebrates are below 100 feet (30 m), with white, feathery black coral trees and sea fans with crinoids. As with the case at Ngemilis, a strong current makes this a different dive, with more open water action.

The "helmet wreck" contains gas masks, saki bottles, and hundreds of helmets.

Mia Tegner hovers under one of the remaining lifeboat davits of the Japanese freighter Iro.

50. HELMET WRECK

DEPTH:	50-100 FEET (15-30 M)
LEVEL:	INTERMEDIATE TO ADVANCED

Personal artifacts are scarce on Palau's wrecks, because they weren't protected from scavengers until recently. One exception is the "helmet wreck," discovered in 1989. Realizing what was already lost, guides began enforcing strict policies against ripping off artifacts. So this wreck still has its cargo, including stacks of helmets, gas masks, saki cups, utensils, and dishes that help you focus on the human aspect. The forward hold contains airplane engines, which were spared the bomb damage of the stern section. It is also filled with large round canisters, either mines or depth charges. Marine growth on this wreck is a bit sparse, perhaps owing to the turbid water. It is located in Koror Harbor, just ten minutes from the Marina Hotel. The wreck is still unidentified.

51. *IRO*

DEPTH:	50-120 FEET (15-36 M)
LEVEL:	INTERMEDIATE TO ADVANCED

The *Iro* is one of Palau's most popular wrecks. A 470-foot (142 m) oil tanker, it has two superstructures which rise from the deck at 80 feet (24 m) to within 20 feet (6 m) of the surface, lending a dramatic scale. These are the most richly decorated parts of the ship, with giant clams attached to the top crossbar. These animals need sunlight for the symbiotic algae in their mantle to photosynthesize, so they are found in shallow water. The fact that these organisms settled and seem to be thriving in the only hospitable spot in the area attests to the adaptability of these creatures. Down below are deck guns on revolving turrets. The wheelhouse is still intact, as are many of the lifeboat davits. The ship's railing forms a frame for the rich marine life covering the deck.

CHAPTER **VII** TRUK

AT A GLANCE

Truk is the major leagues of wreck diving. Not only are these ships amazingly well preserved after more than 50 years on the bottom, many of them have become gardens of marine life, rivaling the richest natural reefs. And underlying it all is a sense of history. During two days of brutal devastation in February 1944, U.S. aircraft sent some 50 Japanese ships to the bottom of the lagoon.

One of the world's largest lagoons, Truk was a major sanctuary of the Japanese fleet during World War II. But by 1944 the tide of war had turned, as the allies' island-hopping campaign moved inexorably westward. Reconnaissance flights in early February alarmed Japanese commander Admiral Koga, and he ordered the warships out of the lagoon. They sailed on February 10, leaving about 60 supply ships and a handful of minor combat vessels. The American attack, code named Operation Hailstorm, began on February 17, 1944, and lasted two days. When it was finished, Truk was effectively out of the war, although it wasn't liberated until after VJ Day.

Truk is everything you've read about and more. Even if you aren't an ardent wreck diver, you will become enthralled by the history and the dramatic presence of these ships. And if you become jaded by ships themselves, the marine life will continue to fascinate and amaze you. Conditions inside the lagoon are ideal for growth of soft corals and other invertebrates. Surrounding the ships is a fantastic variety of fish life, ranging from tiny fairy basslets to gray reef sharks. The deeper wrecks have less marine life, but dramatically convey a sense of the tragedy of war. Some superstructures and steel plates have deteriorated, but like the ruined temples of ancient Rome, this only intensifies the aura of age and history. You can sense the spirits of the men who died there in personal artifacts like boots, binoculars and saki cups. Although most of the ships are freighters and transports, there are also two destroyers, two submarines, and several fighter planes and bombers to explore.

WEATHER

January to April is the dry season, and also the high season. (It's not really dry, there is just less rain.) Visibility is best at that time, over 100 feet (30 m). During the rainy season, about 60 feet (18 m) is normal. Water temperature is in the low 80'sF (27-28°C) all year round; skin suits are sufficient.

The busiest times for Japanese tourists are May, June, and December, but many of them have minimal interest in wrecks and prefer to dive the reefs. From June through August Australians come to escape their winter. Because of the protection of the lagoon, diving is possible year round.

GETTING THERE

Daily air service to Truk is offered by Continental Micronesia, either through its hub in Guam or direct from Honolulu on the Island Hopper. If you combine a trip to Truk with other Micronesian destinations, don't try to do too much on one trip. Time and budget permitting, Truk is worth one to two weeks, split between a live-aboard and a land-based operation.

TRUK OR CHUUK?

Truk, along with Yap, Pohnpei, and Kosrae, is a

The bombed-out Japanese command post on Eten Island reveals solid construction and the awesome power of World War II explosives.

The tranquil grounds of the Blue Lagoon Resort (formerly the Truk Continental Hotel) were built on the site of a former Japanese seaplane base.

A Trukese girls wades with her baby brother in the shallows of Truk Lagoon.

member of the Federated States of Micronesia. When the new constitution was ratified in 1979, the state revived its traditional name, Chuuk (rhymes with nuke), meaning "mountain" in Chuukese. Germany owned these islands before World War I, and because Germans had difficulty pronouncing the name, it was corrupted to Truk. Five generations grew up with that name and most still use it. Today's children will probably be the first in 100 years to call the state by its rightful title.

Despite the gap between their standard of living and ours, people are hospitable and friendly. The only reports of problems are linked to alcohol, and in those cases aggression is usually directed toward other Chuukese.

Local people will work long and hard on projects that have meaning to them, as in clan or family affairs. But when it comes to working for others for money, their work ethic is more relaxed. Most dive guides come from the same clan and hold prestigious, high-paying jobs, so they are generally hard-working and dependable.

Children are Chuuk's future and its greatest dilemma. Over half the population today is under the age of 16. Eighty percent of adults live on subsistence farming and fishing; the vast majority of those employed in the money economy work for the government. The kids are friendly, exuberant, and curious as healthy kids everywhere. Through movies, videos, and observing tourists they have been exposed to western culture, so they want the things that money can buy: cars, clothes and electronic toys. But the money isn't there, and neither are the jobs.

THINGS TO DO ON LAND

Most land-based divers stay at the **Blue Lagoon Resort** (formerly Truk Continental) on **Weno** (formerly Moen) Island, built in the late 1960's by Continental Airlines and recently remodeled and expanded. The site was a wartime seaplane base, later a coconut plantation. Every room has a balcony offering spectacular views of palm trees, the sea, and the islands that are as much a part of the Truk experience as the shipwrecks.

Taxis will take you into town, but a rented car or moped is needed to see the island. The best view of **Weno Harbor** is from a cliffside cave that still houses a **Japanese long-range cannon**. **Xavier High School**, at the northwest end of the island, was once a Japanese communications center. Heavy steel doors have been painted bright red, offsetting the imposing reinforced concrete of the main buildings. This is the most respected high school in Micronesia; 80 percent of its graduates go on to college. Students come from all the islands, must pass rigid tests, and only a limited number are admitted. Support comes from the Jesuits, as well as from the island governments. Although many kids come from homes with problems, once they get there they fit in and achieve. School personnel are always hospitable to visitors, and the views of the lagoon are outstanding.

Eten Island (E ten) is a place for lunch and outgassing breaks on diving days. During the war it was Truk's major fighter base. From the air, it looks like an aircraft carrier because the Japanese cut down its mountain and used the rocks as fill to extend their landing strips. Today the runways are competely overgrown by jungle.

Unlike the high school which escaped heavy damage, the **Japanese command post** on this island was bombed extensively. Once a substantial two-story reinforced concrete stronghold, it looks like a giant foot stepped on the roof and flattened it like a tin can. Rebar protrudes through holes in the sagging concrete. Massive steel doors and window gates are now rusted in position. Holes were melted in some doors by incendiary weapons. Around the structure, jungle vegetation reclaims its territory, reminiscent of Indian temples in a Kipling story.

People live in and around some of the less damaged structures, hanging laundry and cooking. Residents may charge a couple of dollars to go inside, a major source of income in a land with vast unemployment.

Tours of **Dublon Island** (doo BLON) can be set up by special arrangement. In contrast to Weno, Dublon retains a rural flavor, with no paved roads and residents still in close touch with the land and the sea. Japanese military installations include a communications center carved into the side of a mountain, a partially melted gas tank that burned for two weeks after the bombing, and an abandoned hospital that is slowly becoming consumed by the jungle. The only remnant of a once mighty submarine base is the entrance gate.

Because of unpleasant reminders of war, there are fewer Japanese visitors on Truk than on other Micronesian islands. It's not the distance, because Pohnpei, which is a longer trip from Japan, is extremely popular. However, new hotels, golf courses, and casinos are in planning stages, intended to bring more Japanese and their yen to Truk.

The jungle interior is hot and humid, so be sure to drink plenty of water.

KIMIUO AISEK

As a 17-year-old slave laborer for the Japanese, Kimiuo Aisek (KEEM eeo I sek) witnessed the bombing attack from a hidden vantage point. He later became Truk's first diver and discovered many of the shipwrecks we dive

Chuuk diving pioneer Kimiuo Aisek 1927-2001.

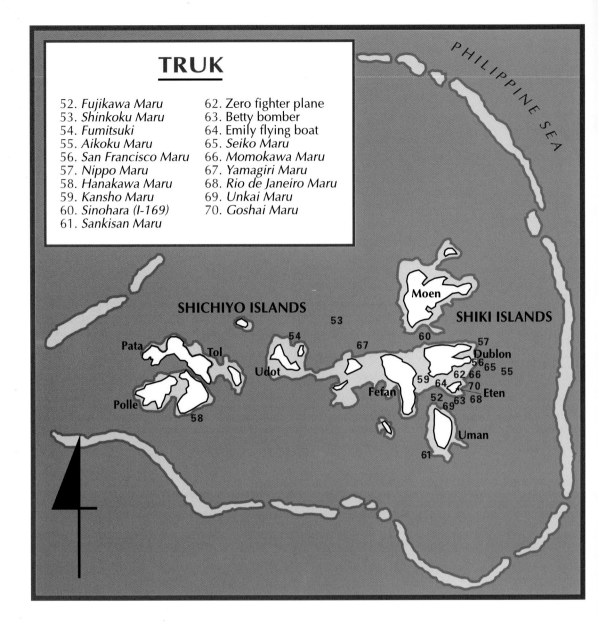

TRUK

52. *Fujikawa Maru*
53. *Shinkoku Maru*
54. *Fumitsuki*
55. *Aikoku Maru*
56. *San Francisco Maru*
57. *Nippo Maru*
58. *Hanakawa Maru*
59. *Kansho Maru*
60. *Sinohara (I-169)*
61. *Sankisan Maru*
62. Zero fighter plane
63. Betty bomber
64. Emily flying boat
65. *Seiko Maru*
66. *Momokawa Maru*
67. *Yamagiri Maru*
68. *Rio de Janeiro Maru*
69. *Unkai Maru*
70. *Goshai Maru*

PHILIPPINE SEA

SHICHIYO ISLANDS

SHIKI ISLANDS

Moen

Pata   Tol

Udot

Polle

Fefan

Dublon

Eten

Uman

today. With an assist from filmmaker Al Giddings, he founded the first sport diving operation on the atoll, Blue Lagoon, now run by his son, Gradvin. A dignified, gentle man with a smile that illuminated a room, Kimiuo is remembered and revered as a tribal chief and an island legend.

DIVING

One prevalent misconception about the wrecks is that all the diving is deep. A Zero fighter plane is located at snorkeling depths and the deck of the one of the most spectacular ships, the *Shinkoku Maru*, is at about 50 feet (15 m). It is possible to enjoy an entire week of live-aboard diving and seldom go deeper than 100 feet (30 m). It's true, however, that some of the well-known wrecks are located in deeper water, and decompression is necessary to explore them properly. When going deep, only two dives a day are possible, with a long surface interval.

Caution. There is no operating recompression chamber on Truk. An accident victim has to be airlifted to Guam. So conservative diving and safety stops are essential.

It's not necessary to do serious penetration to experience the wrecks. Most areas of interest are either on deck or in open holds, or in places where doors and windows are long gone. Guides will take only qualified divers into areas affording no direct exit to daylight.

Operators have differing policies on deep diving. Some allow deep and decompression dives, depending on the visitor's qualifications. Others strictly enforce a 130-foot (39 m) limit, and do not allow decompression diving. This puts certain wrecks, like the *San Francisco Maru*, off limits. Regardless of policy, hang tanks for 15-foot (5 m) safety stops are supplied by most operators.

Diving on Truk can be experienced on a live-aboard or land-based. Most wrecks are within a 30 minute boat ride of the docks at the Blue Lagoon, which are used by all land-based operators. The longest ride is an hour and ten minutes, to the *Hanakawa Maru* and the destroyer *Oyita*. (Only transport and passenger ships carry the designation "Maru.") The advantage of a live-aboard is the ability to dive the remote wrecks and make four dives a day, in addition to night dives. On a typical day aboard the *Truk Aggressor*, the dive deck opens about 7:30. Early risers can have coffee, make a morning dive, then eat breakfast afterward. Lunch is about 12:30, dinner 6:30. People essentially can dive any time they want to, unless the boat is underway. This allows multiple dives on the same ship, including exploration of out-of-the-way places. Night divers must be in the water no later than 7:30. With land-based operations, only four to six divers are on a wreck at once; on a live-aboard it can be up to twenty unless entry times are staggered. The *Thorfinn* is an exception, remaining anchored as a mother ship, while divers travel to different wrecks in skiffs reducing the number of divers on any wreck.

With a land-based operation the routine is to leave the dock about 8:30, make a dive before 10:00, then move to an island for lunch. The pace is casual, lasting a couple of hours to allow plenty of outgassing. Some areas, like Eten Island, offer hikes to wartime structures in the jungle. Others offer snorkeling, as on the 18-foot (6 m) deep Zero fighter plane. Around 1:30 the boat heads for the second dive site, and returns to the dock by 3:00.

Chuukese guides are excellent divers and boat handlers. Their method of finding the wrecks is impressive. The head guide just uses landmarks and dead reckoning, and drops the hook on an exact part of the wreck as though he had a GPS receiver inside his head. On

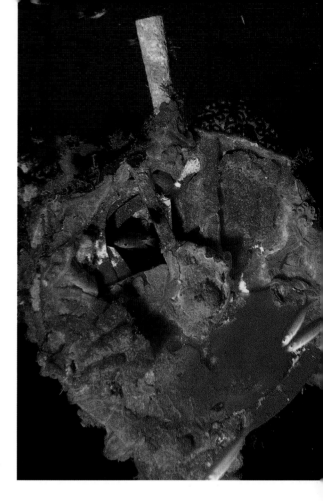

Sponges and other invertebrates encrust the wheelhouse telegraph on the Momokawa Maru.

deeper dives, the guides often carry an extra tank in case a customer needs it. Because the wrecks are inside the protected lagoon, rides are generally smooth.

Truk Lagoon is what's left of an ancient volcano that has sunk over the millennia. Fifteen high, wooded islands are scattered inside; the major ship anchorages for the Japanese were located around four of them: Dublon, Eten, Fefan, and Uman. That's where most of the wrecks are today.

Gardens and Graveyards

The 41 diveable ships in Truk Lagoon fall into two general categories: gardens and graveyards. A garden is a shallow wreck, decorated with prolific soft corals and other colorful invertebrate growth, with lots of fish life. In the open ocean, currents are required for abundant growth of soft corals. In Truk, they are usually located in parts of the lagoon where organic matter drifts down in the form of marine snow, which can adversely affect visibility but provides lots of food for the invertebrates. The beautiful, branching soft corals of the genus *Dendronephthya* are the best in all of Micronesia.

A graveyard is a deep wreck with limited growth that has a more somber, dramatic presence. Some combine the best of both: prolific marine life along with guns, tanks, and personal artifacts.

As rich soft corals and other invertebrates continue to colonize and grow, the personalities of the ships evolve. Some bridges and decks have collapsed as ocean chemistry and weather continue to eat away at the metal.

DIVE SITES

52. *FUJIKAWA MARU*

DEPTH:	BRIDGE:
	40 FEET (12 M)
	DECK:
	60 FEET (18 M)
	HOLDS:
	110 FEET (33 M)
LEVEL:	NOVICE TO
	ADVANCED

It's a tossup between the *Shinkoku* and the *Fujikawa*, a 437-foot (132 m) freighter, for the most popular shallow wreck in Truk. Both share an incredible covering of marine life with spectacular arrays of war machinery and personal artifacts that lend the tragedy a human scale. On the *Fujikawa*, there is a pair of Zero fighter planes in the number two hold at a depth of 80 feet (24 m). One is intact, one only a fuselage, but extra wings and propellers are stacked along the sides. The fuselage still carries a full complement of instruments in the cockpit. Everything is covered with a layer of silt, so it is important to stay off the bottom.

The engine room is huge, easily accessible, and phenomenally well preserved. Entering through an open skylight, you follow the

Inside a wreck, you've got to move carefully to avoid stirring up silt. The pristine machine room of the Fujikawa Maru *looks nearly as it did the day the ship went down.*

stairways and catwalks into a dark hole dominated by massive steam engines and boilers. It's easy to imagine yourself in its bowels, stoking the fires or turning the valves. A machine shop is located next to the engine room, but cannot be found without a guide's assistance. Faint blue daylight disappears as you turn the corner and enter it. Against one wall is a lathe, against the opposite a grinding wheel; a vise is mounted on a workbench, seemingly ready for the crew to come back from lunch. Around another corner is a small storeroom, with shelves of tools and spare parts. Aside from the layer of rust and silt, everything seems neat and undisturbed, ready to be used. The depth is around 60 feet (18 m), but the darkness and the feeling of dependency on the guide makes it seem much deeper. On the way out you swim into the galley, where a huge stove was set up with pots and pans. Next door is the head, with tiled tubs and a row of silt-covered urinals.

In the number four hold is the torpedo hole that sent her down. Steel plates have been bent inward from the force of the explosion; it is big enough to swim through comfortably. Outside, schools of jacks, barracudas, and fusiliers swim around the deck. The smokestack comes within 30 feet (9 m) of the surface and the rear mast almost reaches it. The lifeboat davits are incredible, totally covered with soft corals. One could spend an entire dive just photographing them.

Caution. Penetration is for advanced divers only.

53. SHINKOKU MARU

DEPTH:	BRIDGE:
	40 FEET (12 M)
	DECK:
	70 FEET (21 M)
STERN:	100 FEET (30 M)
LEVEL:	NOVICE TO
	ADVANCED

Even if there wasn't a wreck underneath, the *Shinkoku Maru*'s coral garden alone makes this a magical dive. Below the covering of oceanic life lies a 500-foot (152 m) tanker.

The poopdeck is covered by anemones, so thick it looks like a ski slope. The chain locker, the base of the gun turret, and the lower decks are home to schools of glassy sweepers. These tiny, two-inch (5 cm) fishes form living waves, spilling in and out of crevices as if controlled by a single intelligence. Just under the gun turret is a garden of soft corals, with butterflyfishes, basslets, and wrasses flitting in and out. Even the sides of the ship are covered with a rich growth of soft corals, sea fans, and gorgonians, like a tropical undersea garden. The ship was sunk at anchor, so two anchor chains run from the bow to the sand at 125 feet (38 m), totally covered by the same colorful growth as the hull.

The kingpost on the deck behind the wheelhouse looks like a stanchion of the Golden Gate Bridge. An entire dive can be spent just swimming around it and observing the animals it attracts. Towering some 40 feet (12 m) above the deck, it is covered with colorful sponges, soft corals, sea fans, and molluscs. Schools of baitfish hover around, occasionally under attack by marauding jacks, snappers, tunas, and rainbow runners. On these occasions, the baitfish school splits in panic, then reforms after the predators go through.

Even hard-core wreck divers admit that the major attraction of the *Shinkoku* is its marine

A pair of telegraphs stand watch on the bridge of the Shinkoku Maru.

The entire bow section of the Aikoku Maru *was destroyed in the explosion that sunk ship. Her deck lies at 160 feet (50 m).*

Gas masks and saki bottles are among the artifacts on the destroyer Fumitsuki.

life, both during the day and at night. But the ship itself is well worth exploring. The rectangular windows of the bridge are framed by multi-hued soft corals in shades of gold, purple, pink, and white. Inside are three intact wheelhouse telegraphs, covered with red and yellow sponges and tiny sea fans. Even the compass is still there.

Two levels down is the sick bay, with an operating table, surgical instruments and an autoclave. The galley is full of dishes and cooking utensils. Near the stern, open skylights lead down to the engine room, a maze of catwalks surrounding steam engines built on a gargantuan scale. The torpedo hole that sunk her is on the port side, near the stern.

Guns on the bow and stern still guard the wreck. It is also guarded by gray reef sharks, which are often seen cruising around the stern at depths of about 100 feet (30 m).

54. *FUMITSUKI*

DEPTH:	DECK:
	110 FEET (33 M)
	STERN:
	130 FEET (39 M)
LEVEL:	INTERMEDIATE TO
	ADVANCED

After diving so many transports and freighters, they almost begin to blend in your mind. The *Fumitsuki* is different. A destroyer discovered by Gradvin Aisek in 1987, this sleek, narrow, 320-foot (100 m) long warship seems like a Ferrari among trucks. From the bow, its weaponry clearly defines its purpose: a fixed deck gun surrounded by three torpedo tubes. There is lots of organic snot in the water, a key food source for rich coral growth inside the lagoon. The wrecks with the best invertebrate growth, including the *Fumitsuki*, are located in sections of the lagoon that have this snow of organic matter.

This wreck is compact enough to get a good overall perspective on one or two dives. Contrasting with the pristine condition of most of the ship, the area between the stack and the stern guns is badly damaged. Most of the bridge has collapsed, and now lies on the bottom. Major impressions are the lethal looking, heavily shielded bow and stern guns, and a tall remnant of the bridge structure. Artifacts laid out by the guides included gas masks, binoculars and shoes.

Both propellers are still intact, the port one in the sand, the starboard up in the water column at the end of its external shaft.

55. *AIKOKU MARU*

DEPTH:	BRIDGE:
	130 FEET (39 M)
	DECK:
	160 FEET (50 M)
	HOLDS:
	170 FEET (52 M)
LEVEL:	ADVANCED

A massive explosion engulfed nearly the entire front half of the *Aikoku* (I koku) *Maru*, a 492-foot (149 m) long combination passenger liner and freighter. The blast also destroyed the American plane that dropped the fatal bomb. Looking forward from the triple-decked wheelhouse structure, the sight of the tangled wreckage is eerie, especially in the dark waters on the deck at 160 feet (50 m). On most wrecks you have to search for the damage that sunk it; on this one there is nothing left of the bow except tortured metal.

Some human remains lie inside the stern compartment. A skull is broken into pieces, lying in a bowl along with sheets of parchment with Japanese characters, and the remnants of a wreath. A number of skeletons still remain deep inside the ship, but are left undisturbed out of respect for the dead and for safety of the living. In the galley, bowls, dishes, and bottles are arrayed, along with a pair of spigots.

The stern gun is frozen in a 60 degree firing position, as are the midship guns. Apparently they were firing at aircraft the moment the ship exploded. Marine growth is a lot more sparse on these deeper wrecks, so the firing controls are still readily identifiable. The mast is a reference for finding the ascent line, and also a photo opportunity for wide-angle silhouettes and detailed close-ups of its marine life.

Mia Tegner directs her light to a truck on the deck of the San Francisco Maru at 150 feet (45 m). Chuuk's deepest wreck, its keel lies in nearly 200 feet (61 m) of water.

56. *SAN FRANCISCO MARU*

DEPTH:	BRIDGE:
	130 FEET (39 M)
	DECK;
	150 FEET (45 M)
	HOLDS;
	170 FEET (52 M)
LEVEL:	ADVANCED

Another combination passenger liner and freighter, the *San Francisco Maru* lies in nearly 200 feet (61 m) of water. In contrast to the shallow wrecks, its dark, monochromatic shape seems stark and sinister, the effect perhaps accentuated by a touch of narcosis. Even with decompression, it takes several dives just to see the 385-foot (117 m) long ship superficially, so the best strategy is to pick one section and explore it, then do another part the next dive.

On the bow section, three trucks in a forward hold are surprisingly well preserved. Three tanks are located on the forward deck. They are small, three-man models, but the treads and guns are intact. The forward hold is filled with neatly stacked rows of mines and detonators, still lethal after more than half a century. The deck gun, reportedly the most spectacular in Truk, is mounted on a huge, motorized swivel.

The engine room skylights are framed by four ventilator horns, two of them totally intact. A huge mast, shaped like a cross, looms above the bow with even the rigging overgrown with invertebrate life. Silhouettes of divers on this mast are among the most widely published pictures of Truk. A visit to the San Francisco Maru is exciting because this is a classic wartime shipwreck, both on a grand and an intimate scale.

57. NIPPO MARU

DEPTH:	BRIDGE:
	80 FEET (24 M)
	DECK:
	110 FEET (33 M)
	HOLDS:
	120 FEET (36 M)
LEVEL:	INTERMEDIATE TO
	ADVANCED

The wheelhouse is the outstanding feature of this 352-foot (107 m) long freighter, with the helm and the telegraph virtually intact. The wooden spokes of the steering wheel have rotted away, but the brass frame hangs over the structure, which from one angle resembles a human face. This is one of the most commonly photographed underwater scenes on Truk, but it looks exactly like you would expect the command bridge of a sunken ship to look.

Nippo was a water carrier that also transported wheeled artillery pieces. On the upper deck are ventilator horns, as well as the main smokestack which has broken off and lies horizontally. On the port side of the forward deck is a small tank. Schools of glassy sweepers fill the crevices around the anchor winch. In the forward hold are artillery pieces on wheels, a bomb, mines and cordite fuses.

More mines and bombs are in the rear hold. Among the artifacts set out by guides are bottles, cups, plates, gas masks and batteries. New artifacts continue to be found and put on display.

The descent line is usually tied to the forward mast, so that's the site of the safety decompression stop. In addition to its rich invertebrate growth, groupers hang out there, and you can watch schools of baitfish suddenly part as marauding jacks come swimming through.

58. HANAKAWA MARU

DEPTH:	BRIDGE:
	50 FEET (15 M)
	DECK:
	75 FEET (23 M)
	BOTTOM:
	80 TO 100 FEET
	(24-30 M)
LEVEL:	NOVICE TO
	ADVANCED

One of the more remote wrecks, the freighter *Hanakawa* is usually dived from a live-aboard. According to Gradvin Aisek, it has the best soft corals in the lagoon. The ship burned before it

---

LEAVE THOSE ARTIFACTS ALONE

A law passed in 1972 by the Truk legislature makes it a crime to remove anything from the wrecks. Although the vast majority of divers obey the law, there have been violations, and some visitors have been jailed or fined when a luggage check revealed artifacts. For divers, the best advice regarding artifacts and skeletons is look and photograph, but don't touch. On most of the ships, dive guides have moved artifacts and laid them out in the open where they can easily be seen and photographed. These include items from bullets to saki bottles, helmets, gas masks, a typewriter, and a surgical kit.

sunk, and the wheelhouse structure is heavily damaged and sagging, with some sections looking as though they were melted. This wreck is a 367-foot (111 m) long garden of soft corals. You can hardly make out structures because there are sea fans and other invertebrates growing on everything. The amazing thing is that soft corals of four or five different colors are right next to each other. With all the life on and around the wreck, this is a great dive for close-up photography.

There is a caustic substance in the holds that can burn the skin. As long as you stay out of the holds, there is no problem. In the wheelhouse is a big radio set, but not much else that's recognizable. The forward mast is T-shaped, and covered with rich marine growth, including some spectacular sea fans that make for dramatic silhouettes. The anchor chain is alive with soft corals making it all but unrecognizable.

From a live-aboard, the *Hanakawa* is an excellent night dive. Lionfishes and sleeping groupers are common. Black coral grows from the deck rail, and leather corals dominate the stern deck. A beautiful, well-preserved lantern lies among them. A short, squat deck gun is pointed upward at a 45 degree angle. The *Hanakawa* is more like a living reef than a shipwreck, and well worth the long boat ride.

59. KANSHO MARU

DEPTH:	MAST:
	25 FEET (8 M)
	DECK:
	70 FEET (21 M)
	HOLDS:
	90 FEET (27 M)
LEVEL:	NOVICE TO
	ADVANCED

Another freighter, the *Kansho Maru* was bombed in Kwajalein, then towed to Truk for repairs. Nobody was on board when the 380-foot (115 m) ship sank. She was found by Klaus Lindemann in 1980, so there are more artifacts that haven't been handled or taken over the years. These include a typewriter, binoculars, a

Buckled steel plates attest to the power of the explosives that destroyed the ships of Truk Lagoon.

sextant, lanterns, dishes, bottles and shoes, all laid out on deck where they are easy to spot.

The engine room is easy to enter through an open skylight, with a covering of brown silt over three huge cylinder heads. If you plan to shoot pictures, get there first before everybody's bubbles bring down a rain of debris.

In the wheelhouse is another telegraph. Newcomers to Truk get excited over wheelhouse telegraphs until they realize that most wrecks have beautiful ones. But each one gets duly photographed just the same. The bow gun is overgrown, and provides shelter for tiny blue damsels. Underneath the wheelhouse is the galley, with table legs still in place, but the wood is long gone. The stove is overgrown by marine life, but pots and pans still sit there.

Marine life on this wreck includes soft corals, sponges, sea fans and big anemones housing clownfishes. A strange looking sponge is found here, that seems to be mimicking a sea urchin. It has a yellow siphon and green projections that resemble thick spines.

60. SINOHARA (I-169)

DEPTH:	DECK:
	110 FEET (33 M)
	BOTTOM:
	130 FEET (39 M)
LEVEL:	INTERMEDIATE TO
	ADVANCED

This submarine was the subject of a film made

by Al Giddings in the mid-1970's. At that time, divers went inside the hull to remove the remains of crew members, which were cremated and brought to Japan with military honors. Penetration is no longer allowed.

At first, you may not recognize this as a submarine. The conning tower is reduced to mangled wreckage, with lots of electrical conduits twisted about. The hull is 343 feet (104 m) long, sleek and narrow, and you can see the curve of the ballast tanks. The deck has rotted away but its framework is still intact. Only near the stern does it really look like a sub, with a small A-frame in front of the open rear hatch. One propeller remains; only a shaft is left of the other one. Diving a submarine is an experience, but due to the depth and poor visibility in this part of the lagoon, it is worth only one dive.

61. SANKISAN MARU

DEPTH:	DECK:
	50 FEET (15 M)
	HOLDS:
	80 FEET (24 M)
LEVEL:	NOVICE TO
	ADVANCED

Most of the back half of the 367-foot (111 m freighter *Sankisan* was destroyed by the explosion that sunk her, probably because the rear hold was full of munitions. In its place is a garden of anemones with clownfishes. The cargo was trucks, with rusted remains and spare parts scattered throughout the holds. Probably because of its shallow depth, the vehicles are not very well preserved. Only the chassis remain; the bodywork is gone, but everything is encrusted with beautiful sponges. The forward hold is full of ammunition clips for machine guns.

The beautiful mast comes within 10 feet (3 m) of the surface, and has a rich covering of marine life including oysters, anemones, gorgonians, and soft corals. This is one of Truk's most striking garden wrecks.

A huge bomb crater behind the wreckage leads to the stern section in about 140 feet (42 m) of water. It is upright, with a four-bladed

One hatch of the submarine Sinohara remains open, but penetration diving isn't allowed.

propeller and the rudder still intact. Covered with fire corals, it's a very dramatic sight.

OTHER WRECKS OF NOTE

There is a **Zero fighter plane (62)**, upside down in 18 feet (6 m) of water off Eten Island. Nearby is a **Betty bomber (63)** at 65 feet (20 m), with the forward fuselage still intact, while engines and tail section lie alongside. An **Emily flying boat (64)** is upside down in 50 feet (15 m) off the southern end of Dublon. Additional shipwrecks of interest include the *Seiko Maru* **(65)**, *Momokawa Maru* **(66)**, *Yamagiri Maru* **(67)**, *Rio de Janeiro Maru* **(68)**, *Unkai Maru* **(69)**, and *Goshai Maru* **(70)**.

CHAPTER **VIII** POHNPEI

AT A GLANCE

Pohnpei is a tropical island that meets everybody's idyllic fantasies. It's a high island, with mountains shrouded in rain forest, rising as high as 2,600 feet (788 m). Rivers, streams and waterfalls cascade down to sea level, singing of a jungle paradise. The ruins of a mysterious ancient city lie secluded among mangrove channels near the shore. Passages through the barrier reef provide access for sharks, mantas and other pelagic creatures. It all adds up to an island of striking beauty that has retained a measure of its innocence.

All that greenery requires abundant rain, and Pohnpei's got it. The interior is one of the wettest places on earth, with 400 inches (1026 cm) of rainfall annually. Along the coast it's about half that, but bring wet weather gear.

Allied with Truk, Yap, and Kosrae in the Federated States of Micronesia, Pohnpei is the seat of the FSM's government. Yet Kolonia, the island's capital, retains a small town atmosphere. There is little traffic on the main street, except during morning and evening rush hours for government workers. The pace of life is leisurely, and the people are friendly.

Outside the city, the land is primarily mountain and rain forest, with a few scattered villages. Hikers and campers will find a varied jungle terrain, from mountains and cloud forests to mangrove swamps.

Tourism has not yet made a major impact, so it offers a return to a simpler time. As a diving destination, it shows promise as more spots are being discovered, and is definitely worth a visit if you are in the neighborhood. Located east of Truk, Pohnpei is accessed via Continental Micronesia's Island Hopper.

WEATHER

March through May are the wettest months;

January and February the driest. But rain may fall anytime. Days are typically cloudy with intermittent showers. July through September is high season on Pohnpei, opposite of Palau and Yap. Windy season begins in November and December.

June through August offers the best diving with the calmest water conditions, and moderate precipitation. During the summer, the eastern side of the island is protected, and the west isn't diveable during tradewind season. Pakin Atoll has good diving then, but travel could be rough. Ant Atoll is closer, and may be dived from May through November.

THINGS TO DO ON LAND

The largest, most renowned and enigmatic ancient ruin in Micronesia, if not all of the tropical Pacific, is **Nan Madol** (nan ma DAWL). The site was built between 300 and 800 years ago in the lagoon on the eastern side of Pohnpei. Encompassing 92 artificial islands covering nearly 200 acres (81 ha), it had already been abandoned when the first westerners arrived in 1820. Nobody knows the reason why.

The most dramatic feature is a 25-foot-high (8 m) wall on the island of **Nan Douwas**, built from six-sided volcanic basalt "logs" produced by natural cooling of lava. Up to 25 feet (8 m) long and weighing up to 50 tons (46 mt) each, they are stacked like a log cabin. The ancients had no wheels or pulleys. How the walls were constructed is one of the many mysteries of Nan Madol. Pohnpeian anthropologist Emensio Eperiam doesn't claim it was magic, but with a smile implies some sort of occult knowledge

A close-up of a mushroom coral, Fungia sp., shows its delicate colors. What makes these unique is that they aren't attached to the substrate.

The mysterious ruins of Nan Madol were already abandoned when the first Europeans arrived in the 19th century.

Atop Sokehs Rock, Japanese cannons stand ready for the invasion that never came.

Kapingamarangi Village is noted throughout Micronesia for its exquisite wood carvings.

levitated the stones. Others suggest more mundane techniques like rafts and ramps that the Egyptians used when constructing the Pyramids.

Known as the Venice of the Pacific, Nan Madol was a religious and administrative center. According to oral history its rulers were absolute and cruel, often resorting to torture and even cannibalism to maintain power. They were eventually overthrown, but the site was inhabited for another hundred years afterward.

The best way to see it is by boat at high tide, drifting through the mangrove channels and landing on islands of interest. Many of the old canals are impassable now, but there are plans for dredging and removing some trees to make more islets accessible. The site is too large and passage too difficult to visit more than three or four of them in one day. Tours usually begin at Nan Douawas. Other sites include temples, burial crypts, and pools where turtles were kept for religious ceremonies. Certain islets were devoted to canoe building, funerals, warriors' and servants' homes, coconut processing, and medicine.

A visit to Nan Madol can be combined with a day of diving. Two dive sites are located nearby, and **Joy Island**, a rustic campsite allied with Joy Diving Services, provides an easy jumping-off point.

Some of the finest crafts of Micronesia are made in Pohnpei: the exquisite **hardwood carvings** of **Kapingamarangi Village** (ka PING a mar ANG ee) . Settled by a colony of Polynesians, the town's thatched and corrugated tin shacks have more of an island flavor than the concrete block houses of Kolonia. The art of carving has been passed down through generations and has assumed a distinct Pohnpeian personality. Exported and sold throughout Micronesia, the graceful images of dolphins, manta rays, and sharks carved by the men of "Kapingi" Village seem to be caught in motion. Beautifully detailed models of the outrigger canoes that played a significant role in the history of the islands are also crafted here. No nails or glue are used; everything is lashed together with native materials. Even the sail is woven from pandannus leaves. At the village you can watch these art works being created, and buy them at bargain prices. They'll even ship them home for you.

If you have time for just one jungle hike, a walk up **Sokehs** (SO kez) **Mountain** provides some stunning views. It's a fairly easy slog, although the trail is muddy, with obstacles like fallen logs and branches. Fast climbers can make it to the top in under an hour, slow ones take up to two. On the way, stop for a breathtaking vista of the harbor. Two **Japanese anti-aircraft installations** lie in bunkers on the flattened mountain top, each with a big cannon and smaller guns. The walk is hot and humid, but can be pleasant in a gentle rain.

The overlook on top is absolutely spectacular and well worth the trip. Spread out below you is **Kolonia**, the harbor, and three of the passes through the barrier reef. This is a must-see for the adventurous who have limited time. It can be done in an afternoon after diving.

Pohnpeians are generally friendly and eager to share some aspects of their culture with visitors. This is despite their word for foreigner, "menwai," meaning "sneaky person." It seems 19th century whalers would regularly sneak ashore at night to have their way with the local women.

An important aspect of Pohnpeian life is the **sakau ceremony**. A mildly narcotic beverage made from pepper root, sakau (sa KOW) is considered a holy drink in Ponhpei's tribal society, used in ceremonies and for auspicious occasions. There are several sakau bars in Kolonia where locals and visitors gather to partake.

The drink is very similar to kava, used in Fiji and Polynesia. The root is beaten with rocks on a special flat stone, then water is added and the mixture is strained through hibiscus leaves, giving it a somewhat slimy feel and heightening the effect. Before drinking, you hold the coconut bowl up to the person who offered it, close your eyes, then drink. Sakau looks like dirty dishwater, but the taste resembles a dilute anise. The initial effect is a tingling of the lips and tongue. Consuming subsequent cups induces a mild narcotic effect. This practice dates back over a thousand years, and is a defining aspect of Pohnpeian culture.

The best-known hotel on the island is **The Village**. Built by an American couple, Bob and Patti Arthur, it has attained cult status among expatriates living in Micronesia, who have made it their vacation hideaway. Constructed of native materials, The Village is a series of thatched cottages built on stilts on a cliff with a breathtaking view of the bay. In keeping with the island experience, mosquito nets and ceiling fans take the place of air conditioning in the rooms, each of which has two queen-sized waterbeds. Even if you prefer to stay in town closer to the major dive operations, a sunset drink or dinner at The Village's restaurant is a significant part of the Pohnpei experience.

Structures dating to the Spanish and German occupations still remain in Kolonia. The **Spanish Wall** now forms the boundary of a park and baseball field. Nearby is the shell of a Catholic church, built by the Germans in 1909. The Japanese dismantled part of it to build fortifications; the ghost tower now has ferns growing between the stones.

The island's interior features rich jungle vegetation, along with numerous waterfalls and pools. Many of them are just a short hike from the road, ideal sites for a picnic lunch and swimming. Serious hikes into the interior are also available for physically fit visitors, as well as camping trips for those with more time. For more sedentary tourists, there is a highly regarded cultural show.

The Pohnpeian greeting, "Kaselehlia, (kas a LAY lee a)" has a musical ring. It means both hello and goodbye and is used like Hawaii's "Aloha."

DIVING

Japanese divers on Pohnpei outnumber all others about ten to one, so it's no surprise that the major operations are owned and run by Japanese. The largest are Phoenix Marine Sports, which also has a branch in Kosrae, and Joy Ocean Services. Other operations include Iet Ehu (yet euu) tours, Blue Oyster Tours, and The Village Hotel. They utilize small open boats and cater to small groups. Joy and Phoenix have larger, faster boats capable of trips to the outer atolls. Although they cater primarily to Japanese, Joy welcomes divers of all nationalities.

The island of Pohnpei is surrounded by a barrier reef, transected by 18 channels that connect with the Pacific Ocean. The best local diving is in these channels during tidal currents, so they are often done as drift dives. The same currents that attract a food chain of fishes bring nutrients to the soft corals and large sea fans along the walls. In addition, two offshore atolls, Ant and Pakin, offer excellent wall diving with better visibility.

One reason for so much marine life in the passes is that fishing pressure on Pohnpei is not as severe as some of the other islands. Local people use simple subsistence techniques, with

A pair of visitors enjoy the cooling waters of Kepirohi Falls.

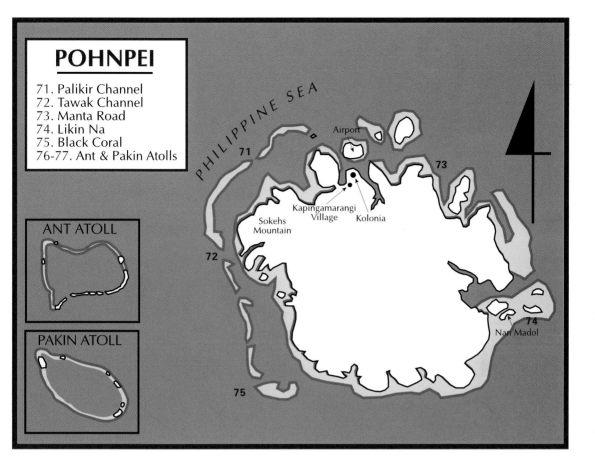

POHNPEI

71. Palikir Channel
72. Tawak Channel
73. Manta Road
74. Likin Na
75. Black Coral
76-77. Ant & Pakin Atolls

ANT ATOLL

PAKIN ATOLL

PHILIPPINE SEA

Airport

Kapingamarangi
Village
Kolonia

Sokehs
Mountain

71

72

73

74
Nan Madol

75

only one line per person, so their impact is slight. The inner twenty miles beyond the reef is reserved for locals only, while foreign fleets from Japan and Taiwan pay big fees for rights from there to the 200 mile (323 km) limit. Their ramshackle fishing boats and factory ships are eyesores in an otherwise picturesque harbor.

DIVE SITES

71. PALIKIR CHANNEL

DEPTH:	30-130 FEET
	(9-39 M)
LEVEL:	INTERMEDIATE TO
	ADVANCED

Located just 15 minutes from the harbor, Palikir (PAL i keer) Channel is a cut through the barrier reef where ocean fishes move in during tidal changes. There are always schools

of fish, which may include barracudas, sharks, mantas, and spotted eagle rays. It's best to dive it on the incoming tide for better visibility and current.

The channel has a sloping gray wall, with schools of fish encountered at various levels and in varying areas along the drift. Whitetip sharks often rest on the sand in deep water. The recommended technique is just to drift along the slope, looking at mid-water for fish, then going out to join the schools.

One of the most fascinating sights at Palikir is a resident school of over a hundred juvenile gray reef sharks. These are small, about 4 to 5 feet (1.5 m) long, and maintain a respectful distance from curious divers. In most areas gray reef sharks are solitary hunters, but juveniles occasionally form roving packs. Three or four adults accompany the pack, as if riding herd on the youngsters.

In mid-water you are likely to encounter schools of barracudas, fusiliers, snappers, and rainbow runners. Barracuda schools consist of big fish, three to four feet long. They aren't at all shy; it's easy to join the school and become enveloped by barracuda.

Don't spend all your time in open water. The reef face is excellent for close-up views of colorful fishes, including clown triggers, bumphead parrotfish, and emperor angels. There are lots of cleaning stations for behavior shots. This is a favorite dive of many operators in Pohnpei because it's close to the harbor. Yet it is also one of the best for guaranteed water column action.

72. TAWAK CHANNEL

DEPTH:	60-100 FEET (18-30 M)
LEVEL:	INTERMEDIATE TO ADVANCED

Another channel cutting through the barrier reef, Tawak (ta WOK) has a ridge running along at 60 feet (18 m) then dropping off. Tawak is a corruption of the Pohnpeian name: Dauahk, which means mangrove. Like the other channels, there is plenty of mid-water action. Several barracuda schools group according to size, sometimes in a circling formation. There are also large schools of black snappers and jacks, with small gray reef sharks patrolling the outside. Some of them

The outrageous clown triggerfish, Balistoides conspicillum, *is one of the most beautiful inhabitants of Micronesia's reefs.*

intermingle with the jacks, but none of the animals seem unusually perturbed.

Many large sea fans line the wall at this site. Reef fish include fairy basslets, angels, butterflies, and a several clownfish species. The wall drops off into extremely deep water, but the best action is shallow. There is little reason to go beyond 100 feet (30 m).

73. MANTA ROAD

DEPTH:	30-80 FEET (9-24 M)
LEVEL:	INTERMEDIATE TO ADVANCED

From December through May, Manta Road offers excellent chances to get up close and personal with manta rays. Between June and November, sightings drop off to about a 30 percent chance. Located near Mwand (mu WAND) Island, this is yet another channel within the barrier reef. It is here that mantas come in to feed and be cleaned, as they do in Yap. At 80 feet (24 m) is a set of twin rocks where divers wait for the animals to appear. It's best to remain low and not chase them; if you just stay there, they will come.

Up to 25 mantas have been spotted on a single dive, although the chances of seeing that many at one time are rare. Prenuptial courtship and cleaning are the most frequently observed activities. They also feed in the channels, but then they are usually cruising near the surface. About 20 individuals are recognized by their markings. Some of these animals are used to people and allow close approach, even letting divers swim above them and look down. The only drawback to this area is visibility. The plankton that attracts the mantas clouds the water to thirty feet and less.

The channel has a sand bottom with a few coral islands. Walls are decorated by soft corals, plume worms, and sponges, including bright orange and yellow varieties. Reef fishes include clownfish and a variety of angels. A colony of garden eels lives in the sand. Gray reef sharks, groupers, bigeyes, and barracudas are also local residents. So even if the mantas don't show up, it's a worthwhile dive for fish photography.

74. LIKIN NA

DEPTH:	20-60 FEET
	(6-18 M)
LEVEL:	NOVICE TO
	ADVANCED

This site is located five minutes from Nan Madol, so a trip there may be combined with a dive. Visibility can be excellent on this outside reef, with antler corals and the usual assortment of reef fish. The slope is gradual, with the best scenery in shallow water. Access is dependent upon weather and tide. If it's rough in the morning or the tide is low, this is sometimes done as a second dive after an initial one at Manta Road. Combining the two sites allows a one to two hour lunch stop at Nan Madol, so it's possible to see the ruins without missing a day of diving.

75. BLACK CORAL

DEPTH:	25-130 FEET
	(8-39 M)
LEVEL:	NOVICE TO
	ADVANCED

Located at the southwest corner of Pohnpei's barrier reef, Black Coral (Kehpara Island) offers the chance of encounters with Napoleon wrasses, sharks, green sea turtles, tunas, or mantas depending on which open water creatures enter the pass. Currents inside the channel can be strong and may even shift directions, but that's what makes this dive unpredictable.

There are also several dive sites on the outside, offering excellent visibility not dependent upon tidal changes. Around the southwest corner is a sloping wall with occasional shelves or steps. From 25 to 65 feet (8-20 m) are sand patches with coral formations which are home to lobsters, nudibranchs, sponges, and shelled molluscs including whelks, cowries, and conches. To the northeast, the wall becomes vertical, dropping from 60 to 130 feet (18-39 m).

Novice divers should stay above 60 feet (18 m). On the walls are soft corals and bright yellow sea fans, along with sweetlips, snappers, groupers. There are also some tunnels and vertical holes to swim through, with as much as 40 feet (12 m) of relief.

76-77. ANT AND PAKIN ATOLLS

DEPTH:	40-130 FEET
	(12-39 M)
LEVEL:	NOVICE TO
	ADVANCED

Diving the outer atolls, Ant (76) and Pakin (77) (pa KEEN), is dependent upon the weather. During tradewind season, November through April, seas are generally too rough to dive anywhere on the west side of the island, including the atolls. In good weather it takes about 90 minutes to cover the 20 miles (32 km) to Pakin, but add another hour for unfavorable conditions. The west side of the atoll is a major drop-off. The east once had a coral point that looked like a big cabbage, but it was badly damaged by a typhoon. Still there are beautiful hard corals and excellent visibility. Pakin has the most pelagics of any Pohnpei site: barracudas, jacks, dogtooth tuna, whitetip and blacktip sharks. September and October are the most favorable months to make the trip.

Uninhabited Ant Atoll (Ahnd in Pohnpeian) is closer, about an hour trip in favorable conditions. A wall on the west side is steep, very deep, with some small soft corals, *Tridacna*, and many small holes and crevices. One cave there resembles the Blue Hole in Palau. Entering through an opening in the top of the reef, you drop through the vertical tunnel to its exit at 50-60 feet (15-18 m). A pass through the atoll's fringing reef has a wall with big colonial orange sponges, along with barracudas, jacks, and sharks swimming in the currents. Blue basslets flit over the corals, while varieties of fishes: clowns, parrots, butterflies, angels, and wrasses inhabit the reef. There are also coronetfish, birdnose wrasses, and bignose unicornfish (*Naso vlamingii*) with a Jimmy Durante schnozz. Lunch breaks take place on white sand beaches where the guides will crack open coconuts for your refreshment.

CHAPTER IX   KOSRAE

AT A GLANCE

A mountain range running down the center of Kosrae (kosh RYE) looks like a well-endowed female in repose, and is responsible for its nickname: Island of the Sleeping Lady. That is appropriate, because this least developed of the FSM's island states is still a quiet backwater where few tourists roam. There are less than 15 miles (24 km) of paved road, gasoline is still sold in roadside stands where fuel is siphoned from 50-gallon (19 dkl) drums, and except for churches, everything closes down on Sunday.

Kosrae isn't for everybody. If you want first class hotels and nightlife, go somewhere else. This island is a trip back to the era when Micronesia was being discovered by the traveling public. It will attract adventurers who enjoy going off the beaten path, exploring jungle and mangroves, and diving clear waters with pristine hard corals.

Until 1992 there was no full-time professional dive operation on the island. Then Pohnpei's Phoenix Marine set up a branch operation. Two years later a pair of Australian couples built the Kosrae Nautilus Resort. A year later an American couple opened Kosrae Village, built in native style along the lines of Pohnpei's Village and Yap's Pathways. This not only established diving, but moved the island's hotel accommodations fifty years beyond existing facilities. Finally there were resorts that could attract an international clientele. Don't expect the Hilton; these are a bit on the rustic side. But that's the charm of Kosrae.

It's still not easy to get around. There are no taxis, so if you want to be independent of the resort's vans, you'll need to rent a car. There are a couple of agencies whose procedures display an island informality. They may not even ask for a driver's license or a credit card until the vehicle is returned. On the other hand, where can you go?

In some places the paved road just ends for a few hundred yards and becomes a potholed, rutted dirt track before resuming. Others can become obstacle courses of mud after one of the island's frequent showers. The main road into **Tofol** (TOE fall), the largest village, is one of these.

Restaurants are small ma and pa operations, with the kind of plastic upholstered furniture that's become fashionable again in today's retro-diners. Prices are low and service is personable, but unhurried.

The ancient Kosraeans were seagoing warriors, who at one time had conquered neighboring Pohnpei. That island's Nan Madol probably influenced the construction of **Lelu** (LAY luh), which was built later and bears a striking resemblance. Foreign whalers and traders made Kosrae a regular stop in the 1820s, introducing their ways as well as their diseases. (Foreigners today are called "ahsit," recalling a favorite expletive of the early visitors.) Within 60 years, the local population had dropped to less than 300.

Congregationalist missionaries did an effective job of converting the few hardy natives who survived the white man's epidemics, so it wasn't long before mid-19th century Congregationalism effectively replaced the tribal culture of the island. It is still the major social force in the lives of today's 7,000 Kosraeans. So even the foreign-run dive operations are forced to keep their boats docked on Sunday.

There is even a law (not strictly enforced) against swimming on the sabbath. Churches always welcome visitors, and the songs of the choirs are gifted and inspiring. But this can be

Brilliant crinoids, Oxycomanthus sp., perch on a coral head in Kosrae's clear waters.

frustrating for tourists with limited vacation time who want to go underwater. With Air Mike flights three days a week, it is possible to arrive in Kosrae on Tuesday, head west on Saturday, and avoid Sunday closures.

Mike Collins, an expatriate from New Zealand, points out a positive side of this situation: "There is an innocence here, a spirit...As outsiders, we can make too big an issue of Sunday, where in the overall scheme of things, perhaps there is something that comes from it that is worthwhile. There is some magic here. This ocean panorama is like nothing else in the FSM. A small, high island, a reef that's very close, some rock that's actually millions of years old...Maybe it's the influence of the sleeping lady, mythologically speaking..."

As U.S. subsidies phase out, the people of Kosrae are turning toward tourism to help develop their economy. Eventually the conflict between the demands of visitors, the church-mandated Sunday closures, and the laid-back island lifestyle will have to be resolved.

WEATHER

Kosrae's topography is primarily rain forest. Rainfall averages 185 to 250 inches (474-641 cm) a year, and is heaviest in summer. The island is located outside the normal typhoon tracks, so heavy storms are rare. The best time for diving is May to November, with no tradewinds and calm water, so you can go to any spot. At other times, diving is limited to the southwest side of the island. Air and water temperatures average around 80 degrees F (27°C) year round.

THINGS TO DO ON LAND

The **Tourist Office** is located in a thatched-roof cabin just outside **Tofol Village**. They can supply maps and brochures to help plan your

A typical gas station is a roadside stand where fuel is dispensed from 50-gallon (18.9 dkl) drums.

A group of Kosraean youths enjoy a pandannus snack on a quiet Sunday afternoon at Lelu ruins.

A young Kosraean wades the fringing reef at low tide, seeking treasures from the sea.

activities, and refer you to people who can help make those plans a reality. Kosrae people are invariably helpful and friendly, so if you go on your own near towns, don't worry about getting lost. The jungle is another story; a guide is needed there.

The **ruins of Lelu** are similar to Pohnpei's Nan Madol, only smaller. The walls are built from the same volcanic basalt columns, but Lelu is built on land instead of artificial islands. No guide is necessary; just hike down a trail behind the Thurston Enterprises store, marked by a hand-painted sign. The ruins are overgrown with jungle, and you'll feel like Indiana Jones exploring a lost city. The structures and walls are surrounded by a swampy canal, which can be crossed on stepping stones. A magnificent banyan tree grows at one of the intersections. Some trails just peter out into undergrowth, but on others the sight and smell of pigsties in the background quickly brings you back to reality.

For a time, the site was ignored by the locals. Trails had become overgrown and strewn with trash. When it became apparent that tourism could boost the island's economy, and that Lelu had the potential of becoming an attraction, it was cleaned up. Guided tours are now available, which include a flower lei and some local fruit.

A notorious visitor of the 1870's was the American pirate Bully Hayes. Legend states he buried treasure on Kosrae, but it has yet to be found. Hayes escaped from prison in Australia, stole a 218-ton (198 mt) brigantine, the *Leonora*, and sailed it to Kosrae. A sudden storm sent it to the bottom of **Utwe Harbor** (OOT way). Although the remains have been pounded by a century of storms and dredging operations, some copper plates and parts of the mast still remain at free diving depths, about 35 feet (11 m). People are discouraged from diving there because of the silty bottom. The **Kosrae Museum**, located in a hundred-year-old warehouse on Lelu Island, has a small exhibit on Hayes, along with charts of the ruins.

Boat trips can be arranged through the **mangrove channels** that wind around the island. Intricate root systems form a latticework above the coffee-colored water while ferns and mosses droop down to the channel's edge. Fish jump out of the water, while monitor lizards slink along the shore. There are three different routes. A maze of narrow canals in the **Okat Channels** (OH cat) form a leafy canopy. The **Utwe/Walung Channel** is wide like a river and leads to **Walung Village**, the most traditional community on the island, which can only be reached by water. A shorter trip is the **Mutunnenea Channel** (moo too NAY neeah), accessed from **Lelu Harbor**. These trips are done at high tide, either in canoes or small powerboats.

If possible, try to do it in a Kosraean outrigger canoe. This is basically a dugout canoe carved from the trunk of a breadfruit tree, very narrow but incredibly stable. Two adults putting all their weight on the gunwale can't even tilt the vessel. Because of its slim profile, the boat slips cleanly and rapidly through the water. Another option is to do it by kayak.

A guide is needed to hike the interior jungle trails. At one time, the tourism office cut a path through the mountains from Lelu to Utwe.

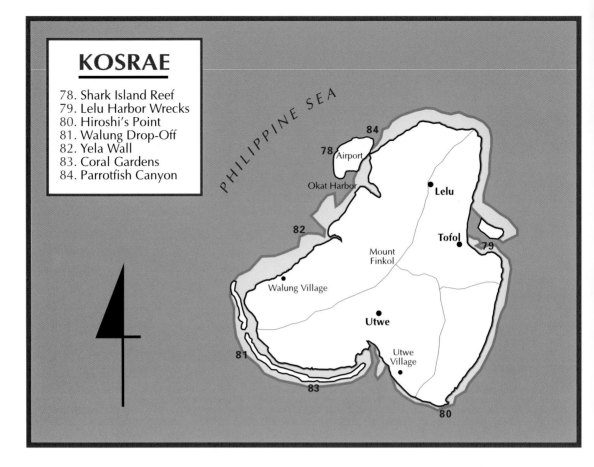

Within two years the jungle overgrew it. The adventurous traveler can climb the **Mount Oma Hiking Trail** to see streams and waterfalls, and a maze of Japanese caves from World War II. Even then, Kosrae was a backwater and was never attacked by Allied forces. It's two hours to the caves, and another two to the peak, with views of most of Kosrae. You will need a guide for this trip and the landowner will be happy to let you in for a price.

Mount Finkol, at 2,064 feet (626 m) the highest point on the island, also has a hiking trail. The first half of the trip follows a river and has little elevation gain. Incredible views of the island and the surrounding reef can be seen from the summit. For the more sedentary, a truck ride over dirt roads will allow you to see some of the mangroves and rain forest. It's beautiful country with tall trees, vines growing everywhere, everything a dazzling green.

Hidden in the jungle are the ruins of two more ancient sites, one in the foothills of Mount Finkol, the other outside of Utwe. The latter, called **Menka Ruins**, is open to visitors.

It was a temple for the goddess Singlaka.

On Sundays, Kosrae Nautilus Resort runs **snorkeling trips** off the beach in front of the hotel and near the airport; **waterfall trips** are also offered. None of these activities seem to bother the church elders, but the dive boats remain at the dock.

The predominant vessels in Kosrae's harbors are fiberglass trimarans that are used primarily for fishing, although **Kosrae Village** utilizes them for diving. Japan's foreign aid subsidized 70 of them in the early 1990's. Recipients had to catch 6,000 pounds (2,727 kg) of fish to pay the fee of $1,000 for the boat, two motors, and full line fishing gear for tuna and bottom fishing. **Phoenix Marine**, which caters primarily to Japanese, and **Kosrae Nautilus** use larger, more conventional dive boats.

DIVING

The waters around Kosrae are exceptionally clear, the delicate hard coral formations are pristine, and the small reef fish seem less spooky than in other places. But the island has had lots of fishing pressure; even turtles and manta rays have been hunted. Three harbors are situated around the island, and there are dive sites near each of them: Lelu to the east, Utwe to the south, and Okat north near the airport. Most of the dive sites are reef areas, but there are also some drop-offs, as the fringing reef drops to 600 feet (182 m) or more.

During December and January, mantas may be observed coming out of Lelu and Okat Harbors. They hang around the entrance in the fresh water runoff, perhaps cleaning themselves of parasites, perhaps mating. Fall is the best time for eagle rays, sometimes flying in formation. Turtle season begins in November, when it's not unusual to see 15 or more on a dive. Tradewinds can make access to the northern sites difficult during the winter, but sites out of Utwe are diveable year round.

Mooring buoys are being installed, 56 sites have been identified, and certain areas designated as marine sanctuaries.

78. SHARK ISLAND REEF

DEPTH:	30-100 FEET
	(9-30 M)
LEVEL:	NOVICE TO
	ADVANCED

This site is just five minutes north of Okat Harbor by boat . The upper reef area, about 30 to 50 feet (9-15 m), has beautiful hard coral formations, with lots of butterflies, grunts, coronetfish, and clownfishes in anemones, as well as leather corals and sea whips. Some mound corals are virtually covered with multi-colored Christmas tree worms. In deeper water along the gradual slope are turtles and whitetip sharks. Surgeonfishes, jacks, and occasional

The exquisite patterns in the mantle of giant clam, Tridacna gigas, are the result of commensal algae that live in its tissues.

tunas hang out in the water column. The reef ends in a vertical drop-off at the point, where numerous reef sharks cruise in the current.

The best time for pelagics is when there is a strong current. You may encounter barracuda schools, eagle rays, trevallies, or Napoleon wrasses. At the end of the point, a converging current from the other side could make the return swim difficult. At these times, this is done as a drift dive.

In shallower water near the airport is a favorite night diving spot, where nocturnal critters come out and parrotfishes sleep in their mucous cocoons.

79. LELU HARBOR WRECKS

DEPTHS:	30 TO 80 FEET
	(9-24 M)
LEVEL:	INTERMEDIATE

Although Kosrae was never attacked during the war, Allied planes made occasional bombing runs, and some wreckage remains. In Lelu Harbor, the remains of a PBY Flying Boat and a Japanese freighter lie on the bottom, along with a 19th century wooden whaling ship.

The PBY is upright and intact except for the engines and propellers. The center gun turret is still there, as is the forward gun along with bullet racks. One wing tip is in 30 feet (9 m) of water, the other rests in 75 feet (23 m). Good buoyancy skills are necessary here because the harbor bottom is silty, and without buoyancy control, visibility can quickly deteriorate.

Some 300 yards (272 m) away is the Japanese freighter, sitting upright in 70 feet (21 m). The starboard side was blown out by American bombers during the closing days of the war. Lifeboat davits are intact, the anchor chain is still coiled, the rudder and propeller are in good shape. Part of the deck has collapsed, allowing divers easy vantage points to see inside the ship. A school of barracudas regularly patrol the wreckage.

The whaling ship lies about 100 feet (30 m) from the freighter, in 50 feet (15 m) of water. It burned to the waterline before sinking. The boilers, tubing, and clay bricks are still scattered around the area, but only the ribs remain from the wooden hull. Near the stern is

a resident group of huge lionfishes. Both shipwrecks are usually combined as one dive.

80. HIROSHI'S POINT

DEPTH:	20-60 FEET
	(6-18 M)
LEVEL:	NOVICE TO
	ADVANCED

Hiroshi's Point is noted for beautiful, pristine hard corals. Plate, table, and antler shapes predominate, especially the plate corals, which extend over a vast area. The most interesting corals and the best diving are around 30 feet (9 m). With currents generally flowing from there to the harbor entrance, a drift dive can be like Alice in Wonderland. Looking up at the reef, plate corals create a staircase effect with outcrops looking like miniature castles.

Among the reef fishes are morays, stingrays, and giant puffers. This can also be done as a beach dive, with a swim of 40 to 50 yards (36-45 m) to the edge of the reef. When currents are strong only advanced divers should dive this site. Just to the west is Issei's Point, with similar scenery.

81. WALUNG DROP-OFF

DEPTHS:	30-130 FEET
	(9-39 M)
LEVELS:	NOVICE TO
	ADVANCED

Located between Okat and Utwe harbors, Walung is the steepest drop-off on Kosrae. The best diving is on the northwest corner, but getting there is weather dependent. At the point the wall drops off into a vertical canyon, with a current funneling across it. Open water schools of jacks and snappers hang out there, with sharks cruising around looking for prey. It's almost like a small-scale version of Palau's Blue Corner.

Shallow areas are covered with finger-shaped corals, with blue basslets hovering around

A Japanese dive guide glides over one of Kosrae's numerous hard coral formations, with scores of Christmas tree worms living on its surface.

Delicate table corals are the best features of Kosrae's shallow reefs.

them. Because of its location in the lee of the island, hard corals are among the best on Kosrae. The typical cast of reef fishes can be found there.

OTHER DIVES OF NOTE

Yela Wall (82), located south of Okat Harbor is another good spot for reef fish. The west side has an abundance of coral varieties, colors, and reef creatures, including dartfish, butterflyfish, angels, and Christmas tree worms. Yellowfin tunas and turtles can occasionally be seen in the area.

Coral Gardens (83) has huge plate and lettuce corals. Triton's trumpet snails, which feed on the crown of thorns starfish, are out even during the daytime. Napoleon wrasses and bumphead parrotfish frequent the area.

Parrotfish Canyon (84), north of Okat, is a shallow reef area patrolled by schools of bumphead parrotfishes. It has been reported that they use their armored foreheads to bump and break coral fragments, then grind them like potato chips, finally clouding the water by defecating coral sand.

CHAPTER **X** MARSHALL ISLANDS

AT A GLANCE

The Marshalls are the sleeping giant of Micronesia. This emerging nation encompasses some 1200 islands in 29 atolls, spread out over 750,000 square miles (1,942,502 sq km) of Pacific Ocean. Development ranges from the commercial and political hub of Majuro (MA jero), one of Micronesia's major municipal centers, to uninhabited jungle islands where yours may be the only human footprint on the clean white sands. Dive sites range from the massive wreck of the aircraft carrier *Saratoga* at Bikini to current-filled passes in Mili Atoll, patrolled by gray reef sharks and other big pelagics.

The Republic of the Marshall Islands is a loose confederation, with tribal chiefs of outlying atolls still making the law in their area. Its economy is primarily dependent upon U.S. aid, including rental for the Kwajalein military base and compensation for the Bikini and Enewetak nuclear tests. As those are being cut back, the nation is seeking new ways to bring in foreign funds and tourism is a leading option.

World War II and its aftermath left its mark on the Marshalls. Wreckage, both topside and underwater, retrace its violent legacy. Divers interested in history and wrecks will be attracted here, as well as those with an exploratory spirit who are willing to put up with some inconvenience in return for being among the first to dive a new site. There are established operations on Majuro and Kwajalein (KWAJ a lin), atolls, a dive resort on Mili, and trips to Arno and Jaluit (JAL oo it) are available by special arrangement.

Then there's Bikini. Site of the post-war nuclear bomb tests, this atoll's lagoon is littered with historic shipwrecks that were opened to sport divers in 1996, making this an instant world class dive destination.

WEATHER

Diving is available year round; some parts of the lagoons are always protected. From the end of October until April there is more wind, averaging 15 to 20 knots. Typhoon season runs during the same time period. They originate here and head west, therefore are not as severe. But on low, flat islands like the Marshalls, the effects can be destructive. The rainy season is from April through June. Summers are hot and humid with occasional showers. Water temperature runs 82-84°F all year round, with air temperature from 75 to 95°F (24-35°C). Visibility ranges from 30 to 60 feet (9-18 m) inside the lagoons, 80 to 100 plus (24-30+ m) outside, with summer better than winter. Winds are strongest in October, sometimes necessitating haul-out of boats.

GETTING THERE

Majuro is 2,200 miles (3,548 km) southwest of Honolulu, about six hours via Continental Micronesia. Kwajalein is an additional half hour flight. Elsewhere within the Marshalls, transportation is provided by Air Marshall Islands (AMI). Between islands they fly 19-seat Dorniers, which can land on anything from crushed coral strips dating back to World War II, to grassy fields that serve as airports in some of the outlying islands. They also do medevac, air-sea rescues, and searches.

AMI agents at some of the outlying islands may be inflexible on baggage weight restrictions. They sometimes weigh the passenger as well as the bags. If you are in a group, equalize weight by trading bags among yourselves to avoid excess charges.

White whip corals and invertebrates decorate the giant chains of the USS Saratoga's bow anchors.

Majuro

Majuro is Micronesia's third busiest urban center, trailing only Guam and Saipan. It's got all the trappings of a bustling city: heavy traffic, supermarkets, banks, factories, and lots of teens hanging out on its gritty streets. The government and business center is comprised of three cities on three islands, connected by a strip of landfill dating back to the war. It's hard to tell where one city ends and the next begins. They are called **Delap** (DE lap), **Uliga** (OO lee ga), and **Djarrit** (JAR it). Locals use their initials, D.U.D., but it isn't considered proper to pronounce the acronym. All told, the road connecting the islands stretches 30 miles (48 km) to Laura Beach. In most places, land is only two or three blocks wide, with lagoon on one side and ocean on the other. The Marshalls are low-lying islands, therefore vulnerable to flooding in heavy storms.

Things to Do on Land

Because tourism is in its infancy in the Marshalls, and this is primarily a commercial and government center, there isn't much for tourists to do on Majuro. But one important place to visit is the **Alele** (a LAY lee) **Museum** (next door to the public library), for its excellent displays on local history. Marshallese navigators are legendary throughout Micronesia. They paddled and sailed throughout the region, piloting by the sun, the stars, but primarily by feeling the direction of the swells against the hull of the canoe. One of today's prime tourist souvenirs is the Marshallese stick chart. Flat sticks represent wave patterns, while small cowry shells stand for atolls. According to tradition, these were the only navigation instruments they needed. A few of the navigators are still around, but they are very old, and the skill will probably die with the last of their generation.

Marshallese arts and crafts are among the best in Micronesia. In addition to stick charts, they make intricate models of traditional outrigger sailing canoes.

Beyond the airport, Majuro takes on a different look: rural, with miles of white sand beaches and scattered homes, a jungle island getaway from the crowding and bustle of the cities. A few luxurious beachfront homes are situated next to simple shacks, but all are surrounded by trees and tropical flowers. It's about an hour drive to the end of the road, but a trip to **Laura Beach** on the western end of the atoll is a journey to a simpler time. American GIs named it after a movie of the 40's, and it has stuck. Laura Beach is a strip of granulated white sand, fringed with palm trees, where you can see the northern islands of **Rongrong**. On weekends, city folks come out here for picnics. The people of Laura sell them baskets made from pandannus leaves, filled with native foods. Visitors are charged one dollar to visit the beaches, which pays for beach clean up.

The **Tide Table Restaurant** at the **RRE Hotel** is the favorite watering hole for visitors, as well as a prime restaurant. Others include the **Outrigger Hotel** and **The Pub**. Cigarettes are extremely prevalent among Marshallese, so don't expect smoke-free dining.

Majuro is a good place to buy needed supplies like batteries or medicines that may not be available on some of the other islands. If you are headed west and have forgotten one of these items, downtown D.U.D. may be the last place to find them until Guam.

The most prominent name in Majuro is the late Robert Reimers, which appears on many of the atoll's major businesses. Reimers founded the commercial dynasty now run by his son, Ramsey. Beginning as a native boatbuilder in the tradition of Marshallese navigators, he established retail trade among the islands after the war. Today Robert Reimers Enterprises (RRE) includes stores, car dealerships, mariculture operations, a fleet of cargo vessels, and a desalination plant. As the largest private business in all of Micronesia they employ over 600 people, which is more than the government of the Marshalls. RRE recently turned its attention to diving, with a center on Majuro, live-in facilities on Mili, and the dive operation on Bikini.

Diving

There are two established dive centers in Majuro, **Marshalls Dive Adventures**, located behind the RRE Hotel, and **Bako Divers** associated with the Outrigger Resort. They each have a dive shop, several fast boats, and can coordinate trips locally or to some outlying atolls. It is best to make reservations in advance, but they usually can accommodate surprise visitors.

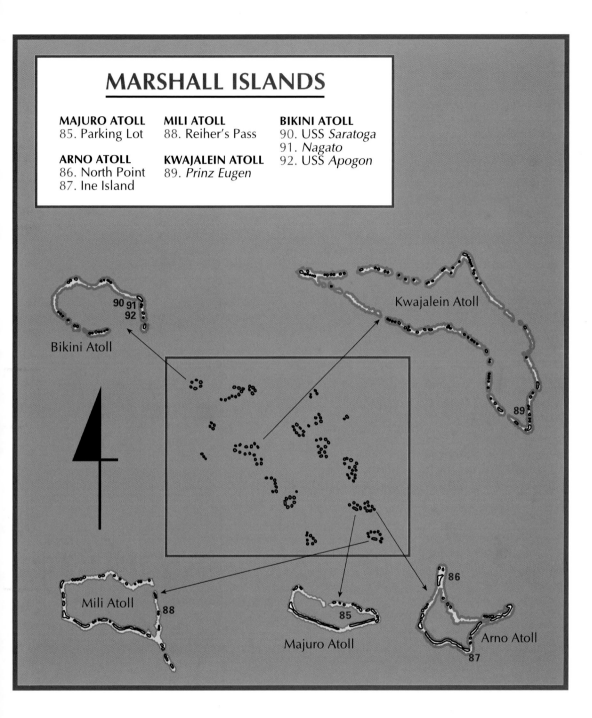

MARSHALL ISLANDS

MAJURO ATOLL
85. Parking Lot

ARNO ATOLL
86. North Point
87. Ine Island

MILI ATOLL
88. Reiher's Pass

KWAJALEIN ATOLL
89. *Prinz Eugen*

BIKINI ATOLL
90. USS *Saratoga*
91. *Nagato*
92. USS *Apogon*

Bikini Atoll

Kwajalein Atoll

Mili Atoll

Majuro Atoll

Arno Atoll

DIVE SITES

85. PARKING LOT

DEPTH:	40 TO 70 FEET
	(12-30 M)
LEVEL:	INTERMEDIATE

At the end of World War II, the U.S. Army attempted to sell its used trucks and jeeps to the Marshallese, who weren't buying. So they loaded them on a barge, took them into the lagoon, and pushed them overboard. About 30 to 40 vehicles are scattered around the bottom over a vast area. About five of the shallow ones are connected by a line, others are deeper. Most are trucks, a few of them tankers, along with several jeeps. Many vehicles are upright, as though parked up to their hubcaps in sand; others lie on their sides. Some have been scavenged, but most steering wheels and engines are still in place. Visibility inside the lagoon is typically about 40 feet (12 m), with lots of organic material in the water. Fish and invertebrate life is excellent: long gray sponges, hard corals, and whip corals, along with moorish idols, damsels, butterflies, and wrasses. At 70 feet (21 m) is a landing craft with steering wheel and propellers still intact. , Fish and invertebrates are thickly clustered around the wreckage, making this a good dive for close-up and wide-angle photography despite mediocre visibility.

ARNO ATOLL

The closest atoll to Majuro, Arno can be reached in an hour boat ride, and is done as a day trip. The northern side is beat up because it gets hit by typhoons. Live corals and color are better to the south.

DIVE SITES

86. NORTH POINT

DEPTH:	50 TO 100 FEET
	(15-30 M)
LEVEL:	INTERMEDIATE TO
	ADVANCED

North Point is a drift dive along a steep, bare wall. It begins with a drop to 100 feet (30 m), where divers wait for gray reef sharks. The sharks are in blue water off the reef, chasing schools of rainbow runners, but guides tease them in by shooting their spear guns against rocks. No baiting or feeding is done. It is best to remain with your back to the reef; trying not to get between the rainbow runners and the sharks. After the shark action is over, divers work their way up to 50 feet (15 m), where the soft corals are at their best. If the current is strong it carries people into open water where the boat picks them up.

87. INE ISLAND

DEPTH:	30 TO 100 FEET
	(9-30 M)
LEVEL:	NOVICE TO
	ADVANCED

Located at the southern end of Arno Atoll, Ine (EE nee) is usually done as the second dive of the day. The outstanding feature is a resident school of barracudas that cruises along the wall. There are hundreds, each about three feet (1 m) long.

This is a wall dive, but the top of the reef is very much alive, with sandy channels, lots of hard corals, anemones and clownfishes. It's an excellent spot for close-up photography. Divers have a choice of a long, relaxed excursion on the shallow reef or going deep for big action. The best diving is above the 100-foot (30 m) mark, and you have to swim away from the wall into blue water to see the barracudas. Gray reef sharks and blacktips may also be seen in this area, as well as occasional

On Mili Atoll, the remains of a Zero fighter plane lie in a bombed-out hangar which has been consumed by the jungle.

dolphins and false killer whales. Be sure to take a compass reading so you can get back to the wall for your safety stop.

MILI ATOLL

Mili Atoll was a major Japanese airbase during World War II. Realizing they couldn't hold the islands, the high command drew a line on the board and told their troops, "Fight and die and we'll remember you for it." After Tarawa and Guadalcanal, Americans had learned it wasn't practical to invade places where Japanese knew they were going to die, so they just let them wither on the vine. Despite 20 months of bombing and harassment, four Marshallese atolls, including Mili, were still in Japanese hands at the end of the war.

Bunkers, coastal guns, and airplane wrecks, both Japanese and American, are still shrouded in Mili's jungle. Some aircraft from the Pearl Harbor raid were dropped off there; most have been bombed into bits and pieces. The twisted metal remains of a hangar, now overgrown with jungle, still houses about a dozen aircraft engines. It requires a guide to find these things.

Discoveries are still being made. In 1994, Matt Holly found the bones of an American pilot next to the wreckage of his P-39 Aircobra. Matt dug a makeshift grave, then informed the United States Government. Six weeks later, a special team was dispatched to return the remains to the U.S. and attempt to identify them. There is also conjecture that Amelia Earhart was a prisoner on Mili after her crash. However, Saipan makes the same claim, as do several other islands in the central Pacific.

The people eke out a basic existence with subsistence farming and fishing, but are friendly and helpful to visitors.

DIVING

Diving is based at the northwest end of the atoll, on **Wau** (Wow) **Island**, the site of a *tridacna* **clam farm** owned by Robert Reimers Enterprises. Six cabins have been built for visiting divers, displaying evidence of ingenuity like solar power, flush toilets, and a shower from an overhead water tank. Dive guides and boat operators come and leave with the guests, while the clam farm personnel take care of land-based details. The social center is the screened-in dining hall, equipped with television and VCR. Farming goes on as usual, whether divers are there or not. Dozens of giant clams lie at snorkeling depths off the beach in front of the complex.

The best feature of diving Mili Atoll is the exploratory feel. In the passes, pelagic fishes act as though divers are a rare occurrence, and approach more closely than at some of the better known destinations. As more diving goes on, new and better sites will be discovered.

DIVE SITES

ENALIK ISLAND

88. REIHER'S PASS

DEPTH:	30 TO 130+ FEET (9-39+ M)
LEVEL:	INTERMEDIATE TO ADVANCED

This is one of the major passes through which boats enter the atoll. The best time to dive is during an incoming tide, when the currents attract sharks and other big animals looking for food, including an occasional marlin. In shallow water, schools of rainbow runners may be stalked by juvenile gray reef sharks. Many of these cute little guys are as short as two feet, just practicing becoming real sharks. So the best part of the dive can be the safety stop in mid-water.

Shallow areas are good for observing reef fish, although the sparse invertebrate cover renders the background primarily gray. Cruising gray reef sharks are common, and giant groupers have occasionally been observed here.

Looking from the lagoon to the ocean, giant sea fans are situated on the wall along the right side. Many are over 6 feet (2 m) across, sharing the space with soft corals and giant clams. The best growth of sea fans is between 50 and 80 feet (15-24 m), although there are also spectacular outcrops bending in the current along the 120- to 130-foot (36-39 m) bottom.

Because of the currents, this should be done as a drift dive. Shallow reef areas are accessible for intermediates; open water and deep areas are strictly advanced territory.

KWAJALEIN ATOLL

The largest atoll in the world, Kwajalein is known in military circles as the World's Largest Catcher's Mitt. That's because intercontinental ballistic missiles from California's Vandenberg Air Force Base impact here, then are recovered and examined. The United States maintains a military base on Kwajalein for this purpose, although the vast majority of workers are civilians. An inordinately large number of them are divers; the base dive club has over 500 members. One reason is that the lagoon is littered with shipwrecks from World War II.

The catch is tourists can't stay on the base. After landing there and enduring a security check, visitors are met by guides from **Kwajalein Atoll Dive Resort,** and taken by boat to the **Anrohasa Hotel** on the neighboring island of **Ebeye** (EE by).

Ebeye Island is the home of Marshallese workers who perform most of the menial work at the base. Because of severe overpopulation and substandard housing, it is known as the Slum of the Pacific. In the midst of a tropical paradise it's sad to see people living like this, with barely a tree growing on crowded lots. People on other Micronesian islands live in similar dwellings, but those are in the jungle, surrounded by trees and flowers and nature and space. Despite this, Ebeye people are invariably gentle, friendly, and honest, with a quiet dignity.

Kids are everywhere, playing with home-made toys. Kites of card-size pieces of Styrofoam plates fly with a tiny tail and string wrapped around a Pepsi can. Baseball is played with cardboard gloves, a tennis ball, and a stick. But basketball is the number one activity. What the kids lack in size they make up in speed, moves, and passes, and better teamwork than the NBA.

Accommodations are basic at the Anrohasa Hotel, but the large rooms are equipped with air conditioning, a small refrigerator, and television with Armed Forces satellite feed. The **Anrohasa** has a good restaurant, and nearby **Bob's** offers excellent seafood.

A new causeway connects Ebeye with the islands to the north: **Loi** (LO ee), **Ebwoj** (EB a waj), and **Gugegwe** (GOO jee goo, a wonderful island name). The goal is to build decent housing on the northern islands, then eventually demolish the shanties on Ebeye. At the present time, there is very little for visitors to do on Ebeye besides dive, unless they are also interested in deep sea fishing. Marlin and tuna are out there all year round. Otherwise a stay of three to four days is adequate.

DIVING

Thirty seven diveable wrecks lie on the bottom of **Kwajalein Lagoon**, the result of repeated bombing attacks during World War II. Twenty eight of them of them are at the southern end, within a 20-minute boat ride from Ebeye. This area is largely unaffected by weather and can be dived at any time. Nine more are at the northern end, near **Roi Namur Islands**. However, the lagoon is 60 miles (97 km) across at its widest point, a long boat ride under any conditions, but especially when it's windy. Furthermore, the route to Roi Namur is closed off for a week or so at a time throughout missile catching season. So those wrecks are usually limited to people living and working on the base.

DIVE SITES

89. *PRINZ EUGEN*

DEPTH:	0 TO 100 FEET
	(0-30 M)
LEVEL:	NOVICE TO
	ADVANCED

One of the best wreck dives in Micronesia, the *Prinz Eugen* (OY gun) projects an aura of history, destruction, and the folly of war. This heavy cruiser was the escort ship of the German battleship *Bismarck*. In the early days of World War II, they sank the British battleship HMS *Hood*, leaving only three survivors out of a crew of 1,400. Afterward the *Eugen* had a checkered career, suffering significant battle damage on three occasions. After Germany and Japan surrendered, the ship was towed to Bikini Atoll, where she survived the Crossroads atomic bomb tests in July, 1946. Damaged but too hot to scrap, she was towed to Kwajalein for observation and long-term testing on the after-effects of radiation.

One of the three giant propellers of the heavy cruiser Prinz Eugen *stands above the surface of Kwajalein Lagoon. Two are still on the ship; the third is in a German museum.*

During late December, 1946, she began taking on water. With only a skeleton crew available during Christmas holidays, it was impossible to stop the leaking. They towed the crippled ship to the vicinity of Ennubuj (EN a booj) Island, where on the morning of December 22, she capsized and sank.

The entire ship is upside down, balanced on its stern superstructure, with one propeller out of the water. Another is just below the surface, where it has become a major photo spot. The third rests in a German museum. The forward half of the hull is suspended off the bottom, with the deepest part of the bow at 70 feet (21 m), hanging over the sand around 30 feet (9 m) below.

Over the years, military and civilian workers on Kwajalein have systematically looted artifacts from the stricken cruiser. Today the wreck is protected by the Marshallese Government, but looting still goes on surreptitiously. Despite this, about two thirds of the original portholes still line the 700-foot (212 m) hull. Some massive deck guns have fallen to the bottom, others are still attached to their turrets, although the upside down orientation makes them hard to identify.

Penetration diving is forbidden and unnecessary, because of the plethora of attractions outside. There isn't a lot of growth, except for some areas of long, thin red sponges

dangling downward like giant candles. Near the stern are the huge gun turrets, along with areas of ladders and gangplanks and jumbled wires. This is also the shallowest area, with the bottom at 40 to 50 feet (12-15 m). Underneath the bow, gray reef sharks often patrol the sand at 100 feet (30 m).

What makes the Prinz Eugen unique is that it's a full-fledged warship with a notorious history. Its upside down orientation lends the entire dive an eerie feeling, and with the hull off the bottom, there are many dimensions to explore.

OTHER DIVES OF NOTE

Other good wreck dives near Ebeye include a **Japanese seaplane**, a pair of **fishing boats** near Loi Island, and a bomber wreck.

Operators sometimes set up **shark dives** inside the lagoon. The guides spear fish, which attracts gray reef sharks and white tips. They use 15-foot (5 m) pole spears to keep fish and sharks away from themselves.

In the ocean near Ebeye there are three areas with different walls. The west side has staghorn corals, on the northwest is a double wall dropping from 20 to 90 feet (6-27 m) into sand, then dropping off again at 90 (27 m). However, with the outstanding wrecks in the atoll, there is little incentive to dive outside the lagoon.

BIKINI ATOLL

The subject of speculation, rumor, and many a diver's fantasy is Bikini, a small northern Marshallese atoll that was blasted into public consciousness in mid century as the site of 23 nuclear bomb tests. In 1946 the U.S. Navy moved out the native population and moved in 242 ships and 42,000 men for Operation Crossroads, the first two blasts. They stripped the lush vegetation of Bikini and Eneu (EN yu) Islands, replacing it with bunkers and quonset huts. The 73 target ships comprised the fifth largest navy in the world at the time. Among them were obsolete U.S. warships as well as captured vessels from Japan and Germany. All were outfitted for combat, containing fuel, bombs, torpedoes and ammunition. Submarines were rigged at various depths to test blast effects underwater.

The first two explosions, Able on July 1 and Baker on July 25, were the only atom bomb tests ever conducted on ships. The weapons were 20 kiloton plutonium bombs like the "Fat Man" that destroyed Nagasaki. Able was an aerial blast dropped from a bomber. Baker was set off 90 feet (27 m) underwater.

Only 14 vessels went down as direct effects of the blasts. Nine additional landing craft were scuttled within days inside the lagoon. But an unexpected menace, radioactivity, contaminated the remaining ships. Despite attempts to scrub, scrape, and repaint the surviving vessels, Geiger counters continued to click wildly. All but nine were subsequently sunk or scrapped.

Fifty years later the ships are free of radioactivity, but pose a different challenge to divers: depth. Their hulls rest 170 to 190 feet (42-58 m) beneath the surface. The most renowned are the USS *Saratoga*, this nation's first fleet aircraft carrier, and the *Nagato*, flagship of Japan's Admiral Yamamoto from which he commanded the attack on Pearl Harbor. The *Nagato* and Germany's *Prinz Eugen* were thought to be symbolic sacrifices, writing a closing chapter of World War II. Other diveable shipwrecks at Bikini include the submarines *Pilotfish* and *Apogon*, the battleship *Arkansas*, the attack transports *Gilliam* and *Carlile*, and the destroyers *Anderson* and *Lamson*.

When bomb testing began, Bikini's population of 167 persons was "temporarily" moved away. Eventually they were resettled on Kili (KILL ee), an island 450 miles (726 km) from Bikini. There are now 2,200 Bikinians; 900 of them reside on Kili living off the proceeds from trust funds wrested from a contrite U.S. government. For 50 years they have longed to return home. Although the island itself is now considered safe to live on, nothing growing there can be eaten because of radioactive contamination from cesium in the soil. The cure is currently the subject of heated debate, and repatriation is still a far-off dream.

As part of reparations, the citizens of Bikini were granted ownership of all the shipwrecks. They contracted with Marshalls Dive Adventures to run a sport diving operation in an effort to generate income for the community, and to show the world that Bikini is no longer contaminated.

Since the tests ended, the U.S. Department of Energy has had a base on Bikini, running studies on radioactivity and its effect on vegetation. Their activities are now limited to November through April, the off-season for diving. Despite gags about two-headed morays, and being able to night dive without lights, the background radiation level on land and underwater is about 1/10 that of any major U.S. city.

Divers fly into Majuro, then on to Bikini the

BIKINI'S LIGHTER SIDE

In 1946, French designers introduced a daring new two-piece swim suit for women. They called it "Atome." After the tests, the press gave it a new name: "Bikini."

Bravo crater is all that's left of two islands, obliterated in the March 1, 1954 hydrogen bomb blast near Nam Island. The resulting crater is 1-1/2 miles (2.4 km) wide and 200 feet (61 m) deep. It's at the opposite end of the atoll from Bikini Island, so ask your pilot to do a flyover on the way in or out.

next day. They are housed in wooden buildings facing the lagoon; each has an air-conditioned, private room with shower and bath. Accommodations are comfortable, but basic. All food is shipped in from Majuro. Visitors have access to the DOE's dining facilities, video theater, and store. Night life is lacking; there's little to do on the island except read or watch a taped movie. But when you walk the beautiful beaches at sunset, you understand why the Bikinians long to return home.

DIVING

The prime challenge to divers at Bikini is depth. The shallowest wreck is the *Saratoga*, with the control tower at 50 feet (15 M), the deck at 100 30 m), and the hangar deck at about 130 (39 m). Most diving on the other wrecks ranges from 130 to 190 feet (39-58 m), with bottom times of 20 to 25 minutes and decompression stops twice that long. The 10- and 20-foot (3-6 m) stops are done on 75 percent oxygen, but computed on air tables. One reason for caution is that the nearest recompression chamber is in Kwajalein, a minimum of four hours away. Obviously, this is a place for advanced and technical divers. But the reward for the travel and the risk is the incredible experience of diving historic warships that have been virtually untouched for half a century. Bikini is a trip back in time that catches you up in the mood and the feel of the past. If you are into wreck diving or war history, it's the trip of a lifetime.

DIVE SITES

90. USS *SARATOGA*

DEPTH:	TOP OF ISLAND:
	40 FEET (12 M)
	STERN KEEL:
	190 FEET (58 M)
LEVEL:	ADVANCED

The only aircraft carrier and the biggest ship anywhere that can be visited by recreational divers, "Old Sara" allows only scratching the surface on three or four dives. Built in 1922 as a cruiser, she was transformed into an aircraft carrier in 1928, the third in the U.S. Navy and the first fleet carrier. The 880-foot (269 m) long ship had a distinguished career; nearly 100,000 landings on her deck was a record at the time. The Saratoga saw action in the Pacific from Wake Island and Guadalcanal to Tarawa and Bougainville. At Iwo Jima she was hit by five kamikazes in one day, killing 123 men.

This vessel really defines a warship; she is bristling with guns. Pairs of five-inch guns on turrets rise above the flight deck; numerous anti-aircraft guns are located in pods outside the hull. The teak deck has long rotted away, but rivets still mark where the boards were located.

Marine life on the wreck is outstanding, with

The island of the Saratoga *towers 60 feet (18 m) over the flight deck.*

Fabio Amaral views a wine glass in the china closet of the Saratoga.

big jacks, unicornfish, fusiliers, puffers, lots of sponges and some hard corals. But for divers that's almost extraneous. Despite bomb damage and 50 years underwater, things that could easily have been taken, like portholes and storm covers, are just lying there. Sinks, radios with knobs and dials, telephones, are all in place, and knobs still turn.

This was the wartime flagship of Admiral Bull Halsey; when you enter the wheelhouse at 60 feet (18 m), you are swimming where he once walked. A subdued, eerie light filters through the slits of the blast covers over the portholes. The compass binnacle, steering helm, and telegraph are intact, although the wheel itself is gone. On the walls are dials, electrical conduits, and all kinds of gauges and controls. It's easy to imagine yourself there at the height of combat.

The hangar deck is accessed at 130 feet (39 m) through the forward aircraft elevator shaft. Just inside is a rack of bombs; beyond are three Helldiver dive bombers and an Avenger torpedo bomber, bent and beat up, but all instruments remain in the cockpits, and the firing button on the control stick is still red. Beyond is a rack of torpedoes, tumbled but not exploded by the force of the sinking. Lines have been placed in the interior of the ship, so it's possible to make guided treks into the combat information center, the officers' barber shop, and the admiral's quarters. These are located at the hangar deck level. Be careful not to stir up silt in these confined quarters.

You could spend a week on the Saratoga and not begin to scratch the surface of this ship's possibilities.

91. NAGATO

DEPTH:	PROPELLERS:
	100 FEET (30 M)
	BRIDGE:
	150 FEET (45)
	GUNS:
	170 FEET (52 M)
LEVEL:	ADVANCED

The most infamous ship in Operation

Crossroads was the Japanese battleship *Nagato*, flagship of Admiral Isoruku Yamamoto from which he commanded the attack on Pearl Harbor. It was from her bridge on the 708-foot-long (215 m) ship that he gave the command, "Climb Mount Nitaki," that launched the attack. Divers today can swim on that bridge, broken away from the hull and lying on its side in 170 feet (52 m).

The *Nagato* saw action in the Aleutians, the Marianas and Leyte Gulf, but was badly damaged and ended the war on a repair dock in Tokyo Bay. She was the only Japanese battleship still afloat at the time. By the time it reached Bikini, the onetime pride of Japan's navy looked like she had already been bombed. She survived the Able blast but Baker sent her to the bottom.

The ship is upside down, which limits its diveablility. The shallowest spot is the stern, at around 100 feet (30 m), where four massive propellers and shafts hint at her power. Below the deck are two of her gigantic 16-inch (41 cm) guns, festooned with a forest of gray whip corals. At 160 feet (50 m), this is the deepest practical part of the wreck, and is usually dived first, before heading up to the props.

The superstructure is a separate dive. Although it's on the bottom to the starboard side at 170 feet (52 m), most of the diving is around the 150-foot (45 m) level. You enter through two large rectangular openings, but in the darkness, limited time, and sideways orientation it is difficult to identify what you're seeing. It's mostly barren walls and jumbled machinery. Souvenir-hunting U.S. sailors made off with lots of artifacts before the bombs dropped.

92. USS APOGON

DEPTH:	CONNING TOWER:
	140 FEET (42 M)
	KEEL:
	180 FEET (55 M)
LEVEL:	ADVANCED

The shadowy silhouette of the submarine USS *Apogon*'s conning tower, completely enveloped by tiny cardinalfishes is one of the

The deck was damaged during a 1946 salvage attempt, but otherwise the ghostly U.S. submarine Apogon looks ready to set sail. The conning tower is usually enveloped by the fishes she was named after, the cardinalfish Apogon gilberti.

most dramatic sights I've ever seen underwater. It's a perfect example of how the sea and 50 years time can take a machine of war, sunk by the greatest destructive force known to man, and transform it into an object of incredible beauty.

One of two submarines sunk by the Baker blast, the 311-foot (94 m) *Apogon* saw action in the Marshalls, Truk, Saipan, and Formosa. For the test she was submerged at 100 feet (30 m), 850 yards (773 m) from the bomb. There is little obvious damage; the tower is virtually intact. Only holes in the hull, some of them from an aborted 1946 salvage attempt, reveal the force of the blast that sunk her.

A 40 mm deck gun points at an imaginary target. At each end of the conning tower are anti-aircraft guns with sighting devices called target bearing transmitters. They look like binoculars attached to a rotating platform; the glass still intact.

Schools of cardinalfish, thousands of tiny fishes about two inches (5 cm)long with silvery transparent bodies, completely envelop the upper section. Appropriately, their scientific name is *Apogon gilberti*. When the sub was christened, nobody dreamed her namesakes would become guardians of her grave.

Unlike the battleships or aircraft carriers which are so vast you have to experience them in sections, a submarine is sleek and compact enough that one can get a feel for the entire vessel. The ethereal presence of this sub in the ghostly light of 150 feet (45 m), with its cloud of sweepers, is a memory that will remain as long as I dive.

APPENDIX 1

DAN Emergency Hotline   (919) 684-8111

In the event of a diving emergency it is recommended that you contact the Divers Alert Netowrk.

Since many of the islands and atolls of Micronesia are far removed from recompression chambers divers should take the extra precaution of using conservative dive profiles.

Divers Alert Network (DAN)

The Divers Alert Network (DAN), a non-profit membership organization associated with Duke University Medical Center, operates a 24-hour Diving Emergency Hotline number (919) 684-8111 (dive emergencies only) to provide divers and physicians with medical advice on treating diving injuries. DAN also operates a Dive Safety and Medical Information Line from 8:30 A.M. to 5 P.M. Eastern Time for non-emergency dive medical inquiries. DAN can also organize air evacuation to a recompression chamber as well as emergency medical evacuation for non-dive-related injuries for members. Since many emergency room physicians do not know how to properly treat diving injuries, it is highly recommended that in the event of an accident, you have the physician consult a DAN doctor specializing in diving medicine.

All DAN members receive $100,000 emergency medical evacuation assistance and a subscription to the dive safety magazine, Alert Diver. New members receive the DAN Dive and Travel Medical Guide and can buy up to $250,000 of dive accident insurance. DAN offers emergency oxygen first-aid training, and provides funding and consulting for recompression chambers worldwide. They also conduct diving research at Duke University Medical Center's Center for Hyperbaric Medicine and Environmental PhysiologyCenter for Hyperbaric Medicine and Environmental Physiology. DAN's address is The Peter B. Bennett Center, 6 West Colony Place, Durham, NC 27705. To join call (800) 446-2671 in the U.S. and Canada or (919) 684-2948.

APPENDIX 2

DIVE OPERATORS

Guam

Double Blue Underwater Photography
790 North Marine Drive.,Suite 795
Upper Tumon, GU 96911
E-mail: doubleblue@kuentos.guam.net
URL: www.doubleblue.com

Professional Sports Divers
P.O. Box 8630
Agat, GU 96928
Tel: (671) 565-3488
Fax: (671) 565-3633
E-mail: psdivers@kuentos.guam.net
URL: www.psdguam.com

Gently Blue Scuba Diving
Holiday Plaza Hotel #2103
1000 San Vitores Road
Tumon, GU 96911
Tel/Fax: (671) 646-0838
E-mail: aki@ite.net

Rainbow Diving Services
P.O. Box 10417
Tamuning, GU
Tel/Fax: (671) 646-6743

Guam Tropical Dive Station
P.O. Box 1649
Hagatna, GU 96932
Tel: (671) 477-2774
Fax: (671) 477-2775
E-mail: gtds@ite.net
URL: www.gtds.com

Real World Diving Services
P.O. Box 2800
Hagatna, GU 96932
Tel: (671) 646-8903
Fax: (671) 646-4957
E-mail: rwdolfin@ite.net
URL: www.rwdiving.com

Micronesian Divers Association, Inc.
856 North Marine Drive
Piti, GU 96925
Tel: (671) 472-6324
Fax: (671) 472-6329
E-mail: mda@mdaguam.com
URL: www.mdaguam.com

Scuba Company
P.O. Box 11901
Tamuning, GU 96931
Tel: (671) 649-3369
Fax: (671) 649-3370
E-mail: scubaco@ite.net

Papalagi Diving
901-C Pale San Vitores Road
Tumon, GU 96911
Tel: (671) 649-3483
Fax: (671) 649-3498

Sunset Surf Club
P.O. Box 9310
Tamuning, GU 96931
Tel: (671) 646-2222
Fax: (671) 646-7665

Northern Marianas

Rota

Dive Rota
P.O. Box 941
Rota, MP 96951
Tel: (670) 532-3377
Fax: (670) 532-3022

52 Club Rota
P.O. Box 1469
Rota, MP 96951
Tel: (670) 532-3483
Fax: (670) 532-3489

Sirena Marine Service Rota
P.O. Box 1340
Rota, MP 96951
Tel: (670) 532-0304
Fax: (670) 532-0305

Tinian

Sea Quest Tinian
P.O. Box 79
Tinian, MP 96952
Tel: (670) 433-0010

Suzuki Diving School
P.O. Box 462
Tinian, MP 96952
Tel: (670) 433-3274
Fax: (670) 433-3245

Saipan

Abracadabra Aquaventures
PPP 322 Caller Box 10000
Saipan, MP 96950
Tel: (670) 233-7234
Fax: (670) 233-7235
E-mail: ejcomfort@saipan.com
URL:
www.abracadabra.saipan.com

Stingray Divers
PPP 373 Box 10000
Saipan, MP 96950
Tel: (670) 233-6100
Fax: (670) 234-3709
E-Mail:
rick.northen@saipan.com
URL:
www.stingraydiverssaipan.com

Yap

Yap Divers
P.O. Box MR
Yap, FM 96943
Tel: (691) 350-2300/2321
Fax: (691) 350-4567/4110
E-mail:
yapdivers@mantaray.com
URL: www.mantaray.com

Nature's Way
P.O. Box 238
Yap, FM 96943
Tel: (691) 350-2542/3407

Beyond the Reef Charters
P.O. Box 609
Yap, FM 96943
Tel: (691) 350-3483
Fax: (691) 350-3733

Palau

Neco Marine Corporation
P.O. Box 129
Koror, Palau 96940
Tel: (680) 488-1755/2009
Fax: (680) 488-3014
E-mail:
necomarine@palaunet.com

Palau Diving Center, Carp Corporation
P.O. Box 5
Koror, Palau 96940
Tel: (680) 488-2978/5177
Fax: (680) 488-3155
E-mail: carpcorp@palaunet.com

Splash Diving Center
P.O. Box 847
Koror, Palau 96940
Tel: (680) 488-2600 Ext. 485
Fax: (680) 488 1741/1601
E-mail: splash@palaunet.com

Fish 'n Fins
P.O. Box 142
Koror, Palau 96940
Tel: (680) 488-2637
Fax: (680) 488-5418
E-mail: fishnfin@palaunet.com
URL: www.fishnfins.com

The Perfect Point
dba Southern Marine Divers
P.O. Box 1598
Koror, Palau 96940
Tel: (680) 488-2345
Fax: (680) 488-3128

Paradise Divers, Ltd.
P.O. Box 1287
Koror, Palau 96940
Tel: (680) 488-5008
Fax: (680) 488-5008
E-mail:
paradisedivers@palaunet.com
URL: www.big-dream.com/
palau

Peleliu Divers
P.O. Box 8071
Koror, Palau 96940
Tel/Fax: (680) 345-1058
Fax: (680) 488-1725
E-mail: pdivers@palaunet.com
URL: www.plaza16.mbn. or.jp/
~palau/pdivers.htm

Sam's Tours
P.O. Box 428
Koror, Palau 96940
Tel: (680) 488-1062
Fax: (680) 488-5003
E-mail: samstour@palaunet.com
URL: www.samstours.com

Liveaboards

Sun Dancer II
P.O Box 487
Koror, Palau 96940
Tel: (680) 488-3983
Fax: (680) 488-3983
E-mail: dancer@palaunet.com
URL: www.peterhughes.com

Lesson II Palau Sport
P.O. Box 1455
Koror, Palau 96940
Tel: (680) 488-1120
Fax: (680) 488-1125

Ocean Hunter
P.O. Box 964
Koror, Palau 96940
Tel: (680) 488-3626
Fax: (680) 488-5326/1725
E-mail:
ocean.hunter@palaunet.com
URL: www.fishnfins.com

Palau Aggressor II
P.O. Box 1714-P106
Koror, Palau 96940
Tel: (680) 488-6075
Fax: (680) 488-6076
E-mail:
paggressor@palaunet.com URL:
www.aggressor.com

Big Blue Explorer
Explorer Live Aboards
11602 Bos St.
Ceritos, CA 90703
Tel: (877) 348-3475
Fax: (562) 809-7300

Truk

Blue Lagoon Dive Shop
P.O. Box 429
Weno, Chuuk, FM 96942
Tel: (691) 330-2796

Ghost Fleet Dive Shop
P.O. Box 295
Weno, Chuuk, FM 96942
Tel: (691) 330-2724
Telex: (729) 6831

Micronesia Aquatics of Truk Lagoon
P.O. Box 57
Weno, Chuuk, FM 96942
Tel: (691) 330-2204
Fax: (691) 330-2777

Sundance Tours & Dive Shop
P.O. Box 85
Weno, Chuuk, FM 96942
Tel: (691) 330-4234
Fax: (691) 330-4334

Rananim Dive Shop
P.O. Box 26
Weno, Chuuk, FM 96942
Tel: (691) 330-2470

Liveaboards

SS Thorfinn
c/o Seaward Holidays
Micronesia, Inc.
P.O. Box 1086
Weno, Chuuk, FM 96942
Tel: (691) 330-3040
Fax: (691) 330-4253
E-mail: seaward@mail.fm

Truk Aggressor
P.O. Box 1470
Morgan City, LA 70381
Tel: (504) 385-2628
Fax: (504) 384-0817
E-mail: info@aggressor.com

Truk Odyssey
c/oOdyssey Adventures
4417 Beach Blvd., Ste. 200
Jacksonville, FL 32207
Tel: (800) 757-5396; (904) 346-3766
Fax: (904) 346-0664
E-mail: info@trukodyssey.com

Pohnpei

Iet Ehu Tours
P.O. Box 559
Koloni, Pohnpei, FM 96941
Tel: (691) 320-2959
Fax: (691) 320-2968

Joy Ocean Service
P.O. Box 484
Kolonia, Pohnpei, FM 96941
Tel: (691) 320-2447
Fax: (691) 320-2478

Phoenix Marine Sports Club
P.O. Box 387
Kolonia, Pohnpei, FM 96941
Tel: (691) 320-2362/2363 Fax:
(691) 320-2364

Kosrae

Dive Kosrae
P.O. Box 24
Lelu, Kosrae, FM 96944
Tel: (691) 370-3062
Fax: (691) 370-231313

Dive Caroline
P.O. Box 6
Tafunsak, Kosrae, FM 96944
Tel: (691) 370-3239
Fax: (691) 370-2109

Kosrae Nautilus
P.O. Box 135
Lelu, Kosrae, FM 96944
Tel: (691) 370-3567
Fax: (691) 370-3568

Sleeping Lady Divers
P.O. Box 399
Lelu, Kosrae, FM 96944
Tel: (691) 370-3483
Fax: (691) 370-5839

Phoenix Marine Sports Club
P.O. Box PHM
Lelu, Kosrae, FM 96944
Tel: (691) 370-3100
Fax: (691) 370-3509

Marshall Islands

Marshalls Dive Adventures
P.O. Box 1
Majuro, MH 96960
Tel: (692) 625-3250
Fax: (692) 625-3505
E-mail: rreadmin@ntamar.com
Atolls of operation: Majuro, Arno, Mili, Bikini

Bako Divers of Majuro Atoll
Outrigger Marshall Islands
Resort
PO Box 1818
Majuro, MH 96960
Tel: 011-(692)-625-2525
Fax: 011-(692)-625-2500
E-mail: jerryr@ntamar.com
Atolls of operation: Majuro, Arno

Kwajalein Atoll Dive Resort
P.O. Box 5159
Ebeye, Kwajalein, MH 96970
Tel: (692) 329-3100/329-3102/329-1220
Fax: (692) 329-3297
Atolls of operation: Kwajalein

INDEX

A **boldface** page number denotes a picture caption.
An underlined page number indicates detailed treatment.